W9-AYS-553
3 1230 00880 1132

PRAYERS

THAT

CHANGED

HIST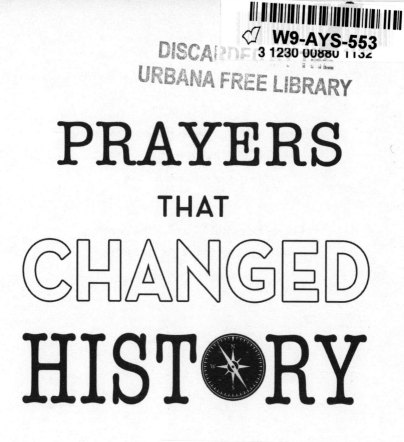RY

There is nothing new in the world except
the history that you do not know.

—Harry S. Truman

Prayer does not fit us for the greater
work; prayer is the greater work.

—Oswald Chambers

PRAYERS

THAT

CHANGED

HIST⊙RY

**From Christopher Columbus
to Helen Keller, how God used
25 people to change the world**

TRICIA GOYER

ZONDERKIDZ

Prayers that Changed History
Copyright © 2015 by Tricia Goyer

Requests for information should be addressed to:
Zonderkidz, 3900 Sparks Drive SE, Grand Rapids, MI 49546

ISBN 978-0-310-74801-4

Published in association with the Books & Such Literary Management, attention: Janet Kobobel Grand, 52 Mission Circle, Suite 122, PMB 170 Santa Rosa, California 95409-5370, www.booksandsuch.com.

Cover design: Cindy Davis
Globe image: © iris 42/Shutterstock
Interior design: Kait Lamphere

Printed in the United States of America

15 16 17 18 19 20 /DCI/ 20 19 18 17 16 15 14 13 12 11 10 9 8 7 6 5 4 3 2 1

TABLE OF CONTENTS

FROM THE AUTHOR

I first got the idea for this book in 1999, and it's been simmering ever since. As a homeschooling mom and a Christian, I kept coming across these great stories of prayer, and I loved them! They encouraged my own prayer life, and I wished there was a resource for my own kids. I believe in prayer with all of my heart. I believe prayer changes history. Sometimes the answered prayers are small. Sometimes they are huge.

The Bible is filled with amazing stories of what happens when people pray: the sun standing still, the walls of Jericho falling, the mouths of lions closing. We know those *are* answers to prayer because the Bible gives us an eternal perspective. We see these events from God's perspective and sometimes we can get other glimpses of prayer-at-work through historical stories and figures. (That is my desire for this book!)

I wrote this book to:

- highlight a historical person and a moment of prayer;
- to teach kids how to pray;
- and to discuss prayers through the very words of the people highlighted. (We do not have God's point of view in these stories, but we have the view point of

the people [or nation] who prayed, and in their eyes
miracles *did* happen.)

As readers of faith, you and I believe in the value and
the power of prayer. This is the lens through which we see
historical events. This is how the people who prayed saw
them. We view history in the way we see the Bible—as a
platform for God to do his great work, starting first in the
hearts of men and women and then through events and
circumstances.

INTRODUCTION

TRICIA GOYER

Over 2,000 years ago, Jesus gathered a small group of his believers together. He had something important to share. It was time for him to return to heaven, and he had one last, important instruction for those gathered:

> *Therefore, go and make disciples of all the nations, baptizing them in the name of the Father and the Son and the Holy Spirit. Teach these new disciples to obey all the commands I have given you. And be sure of this: I am with you always, even to the end of the age.*
>
> *—Matthew 28:19–20 (NLT)*

For the last 2,000 years, men and women who love Jesus have gladly served him. They have gone out into their neighborhoods, towns, and the world, and Jesus has been with them. He hasn't physically walked by their side. Instead, his Holy Spirit has been within them, leading and guiding them. We can do the same. Each of us has a special connection with the Holy Spirit when we go before God in prayer. Through prayer we can make a difference in the world we live in, too.

This book is a collection of stories about prayer. You will read about real people who walked with God. They prayed to him, and they saw things change. At the time, their prayers may have seemed small. Now, many years later, we can see how their prayers and the actions they took as believers changed history. Some men and women like Constantine and Mother Teresa impacted changes in government or set up ministries to serve the poor. Others like Dietrich Bonhoeffer didn't appear to make huge changes in their lifetimes, but they continue to inspire generations. Their humble prayers impacted their lives and the lives of others. Their stories and prayers can continue to bring about change in *our* histories, too, if we choose to get on our knees.

Your prayers can change everything too

If you have Jesus in your life, he is with you always. His Spirit goes with you wherever you go. When you pray, you have a special connection with Jesus through the Holy Spirit.

In this book, you'll learn a lot about praying. Praying is talking to God. Praying is asking him for a certain thing. Praying is letting God change your heart to match his. Praying can be done anytime, anywhere. The more we pray with the right heart, the more we are changed. The more we are changed, the more we impact the world. Prayer changes things, starting with us. When we pray, our prayers can also change history.

Sometimes the answers to your prayers can be seen right away. Sometimes the answers won't be seen for a long, long time.

As you read each story, ask yourself, "What would have happened if this person hadn't prayed and acted on their calling?" Would peoples' lives be different? Prayers of ordinary people opened the doors to God's work. And your prayers can do the same.

Another thing to ask is, "What can happen when I pray?" That's a wonderful question. You'll never know what can happen when you pray, but the results are often bigger than you can imagine.

What happened when godly people prayed? Get ready to find out.

What will happen with you pray? You'll never know until you try.

CHAPTER 1

POLYCARP

When Good Comes From Evil

Mary Evans Picture Library

When He Lived: ca. 69–155 AD

→ 155 AD

Polycarp would rather face death than worship a false God

The sound of men's shouts filled the air. Polycarp struggled forward toward the upper window. He couldn't see much more than shapes in the dim light. His vision had failed in his old age, but the memories of those from his past were strong—especially the memory of John, one of the disciples of Jesus. Polycarp was one of the last Christians alive who had been taught by one of Jesus' disciples.

Polycarp closed his eyes and could still picture the older man's gentle gaze, filled with grace. How had time passed so quickly? Polycarp had been young as he sat under John's teaching, and now he was an old man himself.

All his life he'd tried to follow God's laws, and that

was the problem. His arrest was a direct result of his Christian beliefs. For years, Smyrna (present-day Izmir in Turkey) was a peaceful city, and both Christians and non-Christians lived together without incident. But eventually citizens started to complain. People feared and hated the Christians. Soldiers began to hunt them and bring them before the judges of Rome.[1]

"These Christians do not honor the emperor! They do not serve our gods. They follow their own ways," the people cried.

Polycarp had been the bishop of Smyrna, and soon soldiers began hunting him. They found him in a farmhouse outside of town.

One of the soldiers pounded on the door. "Where is Polycarp?"

Polycarp came down the stairs. "Here I am."

The soldiers rushed through the door.

"You've come a long way," Polycarp said. To the soldiers' surprise, he invited them in to eat.

Polycarp knew the men had come to take him away. "Would you give me one hour to pray for those I love?" Polycarp asked the soldiers.

"Yes," an officer said. "I will allow that."

Polycarp returned to his room and sank to his knees. The wood floor made his knees ache, but his heart ached even more. He thought of the church. He thought of the believers who sacrificed so much for their faith. He asked God to protect them. He prayed they would stay strong even surrounded by sadness, loss, and threats.

The next day Polycarp was brought to the arena. It was a gathering place for the people of Smyrna. There they watched sports events and chariot races. Gladiators battled fierce lions and each other, but this night the audience had come for a different reason.

Polycarp stood in a holding cell. He prayed as he heard fellow believers being led into the arena. When they refused to offer incense to Caesar, as a loyal oath, he heard their deaths at the jaws of enraged lions.

Before long, Polycarp stood before the Roman proconsul (governor) himself. He was being charged as a traitor. An old man, Polycarp struggled to stay on his feet. He could see pity in the proconsul's eyes.

Observers shouted and cursed him, but the proconsul's gaze was fixed on Polycarp's face. "I will release you," he said. "You simply have to declare, 'Caesar is Lord' and offer a pinch of incense on the fire as a sacrifice."

Polycarp squared his shoulders. To the non-Christians, this seemed like a simple act, but Polycarp knew that by making this declaration he was breaking the First Commandment. The First Commandment said there should be no other Gods before the one true God.

The word "Lord" referred to divinity, being like a god. The people saw the emperor as their lord, and they wanted Polycarp to do the same.

Polycarp stood silent. The people called the Emperor Domitian "Dominus et Deus noster" ("Our Lord and God") by his request. But the emperor was not Polycarp's lord; Jesus Christ was.

"It is just one pinch of incense. Surely you can do this one small act," the Roman governor pleaded.

Polycarp had turned to the Lord Jesus many times in

prayer, and he needed him again. He fixed his eyes on the proconsul.

"Eighty-six years I have served Christ, and he never did me any wrong. How can I blaspheme my King who has saved me?"

Polycarp knew what his refusal to compromise his faith meant. The judge signaled the herald. The herald turned to face the crowd. "Polycarp has proclaimed himself a Christian!"

Polycarp's knees trembled, but his heart stood strong. He would be burned at the stake for his beliefs.

His arms ached as he was tied to the stake. And then he lifted his face to the sky in prayer.

Lord God Almighty, Father of your blessed and beloved child Jesus Christ, through whom we have received knowledge of you, God of angels and hosts and all creation, and of the whole race of the upright who live in your presence: I bless you that you have thought me worthy of this day and hour, to be numbered among the martyrs and share in the cup of Christ, for resurrection to eternal life, for soul and body in the incorruptibility of the Holy Spirit. Among them may I be accepted before you today, as a rich and acceptable sacrifice, just as you, the faithful and true God, have prepared and foreshown and brought about. For this reason and for all things I praise you, I bless you, I glorify you, through the eternal heavenly high priest Jesus Christ, your beloved child, through whom be glory to you, with him and the Holy Spirit, now and for the ages to come. Amen.[2]

A fellow Christian heard Polycarp's prayer and wrote it down. The prayer of Polycarp, and his declaration before the Roman proconsul, went from church to church.

From that time on, believers, many of whom also gave their lives for the church, have honored Polycarp every year on February 23. Over the next 150 years, many men, women, and children decided to follow the faithful example of the bishop of Smyrna. They decided to die rather than deny Christ as their Lord, and history was forever changed.

Sometimes Jesus asks us to give everything

Imagine the people who were able to sit at the feet of the apostles. Can you guess the questions they asked of those who shared their life with Jesus—those who had walked with him, touched him, and heard his words of hope?

It might have been exciting for Polycarp to meet the Apostle John, but John's messages most likely weren't easy to hear. John did get to walk with Jesus, but he also faced hardship because of his beliefs. In his gospel, John even wrote that we should expect hardship too. He is quoting Jesus here: "Remember what I told you: 'A servant is not greater than his master.' If they persecuted me, they will persecute you also" (John 15:20).

In our lives, we might face hard situations because of our belief in Jesus. We might be teased or we might have to walk away from movies or television programs that go against our beliefs. When that happens, we can think of Polycarp. Yes, it might be hard to be embarrassed or to stand out from the crowd, but believers like Polycarp were willing to give so much more. Many gave their lives for their faith. We most likely won't be asked to give our lives, but Polycarp's story is a good reminder that Jesus can be with us during every hardship when we pray.

Something to Think About

During Polycarp's day, people were killed for standing up for their Christian beliefs. How can hearing the stories of Christians who sacrificed everything help us today? What can help you stand up to challenges in your life?

In His Own Words

Like many of Jesus' disciples, Polycarp wrote letters to the Christian churches. And just as he encouraged others to do, the time came for Polycarp to stand firm for his faith. In his *Letter to the Philippians*, he said "Stand fast, therefore, in this conduct and follow the example of the Lord, 'firm and unchangeable in faith, lovers of the brotherhood, loving each other, united in truth,' helping each other with the mildness of the Lord, despising no man."[3]

How He Changed History

Polycarp's arrest, his refusal to deny Christ, and his martyrdom (dying for his faith) happened as Christianity became more popular in Rome. The Roman emperor saw the growing numbers of Christians and it worried him. It was a threat to the Roman way of life. Polycarp's death, along with those of others, made the church stronger as Christians came together in prayer and support.[4] Christianity also grew as people who saw their bravery and commitment knew there must be something valuable in this new religion. For centuries, Polycarp has been an example of a Christian who did not back down from his beliefs and who believed to the end.

it's in the Bible

Stephen is another example of true faithfulness to God. Stephen was a believer of Jesus Christ, and he did wonderful miracles in Jesus' name. The religious leaders were angry and they brought Stephen before them. Stephen's words about Jesus made them so mad that they killed him. Yet before his death he had a special message to share.

> They grabbed Stephen and took him before the High Council. They put forward their bribed witnesses to testify: "This man talks nonstop against this Holy Place and God's Law. We even heard him say that Jesus of Nazareth would tear this place down and throw out all the customs Moses gave us."
>
> As all those who sat on the High Council looked at Stephen, they found they couldn't take their eyes off him—his face was like the face of an angel!
>
> Then the Chief Priest said, "What do you have to say for yourself?"   —Acts 6:12—7:1 (MSG)

Stephen went on to tell the High Counsel about all those in Hebrew history who had been mistreated for their faith. Then he continued:

> "Your ancestors killed anyone who dared talk about the coming of the Just One. And you've kept up the family tradition—traitors and murderers, all of you. You had

*God's Law handed to you by angels—gift-wrapped!—
and you squandered it!"*

*At that point they went wild, a rioting mob of catcalls
and whistles and invective. But Stephen, full of the Holy
Spirit, hardly noticed—he only had eyes for God, whom
he saw in all his glory with Jesus standing at his side. He
said, "Oh! I see heaven wide open and the Son of Man
standing at God's side!"*

*Yelling and hissing, the mob drowned him out. Now
in full stampede, they dragged him out of town and pelted
him with rocks. The ringleaders took off their coats and
asked a young man named Saul to watch them.*

*As the rocks rained down, Stephen prayed, "Master
Jesus, take my life." Then he knelt down, praying loud
enough for everyone to hear, "Master, don't blame them
for this sin"—his last words. Then he died.*

—Acts 7:52–59 (MSG)

There are Christian believers like Polycarp and Stephen
who gave everything—even their lives—as followers of
Jesus. It is sad to know the price they had to pay, but their
love for Jesus is an example for us all. Even Stephen's last
words were a prayer to God, "Master, don't blame them
for this sin." He was praying for those who were taking his
life. Jesus said something similar while he was hanging on
the cross: "Father, forgive them, for they do not know what
they are doing" (Luke 23:34). God's love shone through
Stephen even then.

Your Life

There may come a time when people will turn against you because of your faith. It's easier to treat them badly, like they're treating you, but Jesus asks us to do things differently. When we treat others with love, even when they mistreat us, it's a good example to everyone who watches. Others will see God at work in our lives, and perhaps they'll learn to trust Jesus too.

And when you face hard situations, you don't have to do it alone. Pray to God and ask him for strength. He is faithful and will help you stay strong. Trust him in that.

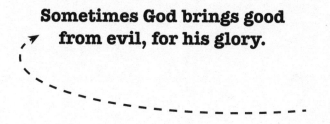

Sometimes God brings good from evil, for his glory.

CHAPTER 2

CONSTANTINE

God Always Wins

When He Lived: 272-337 AD

→ 312 AD

Constantine defeats his enemy

The Roman Empire was divided. Many leaders and different families had produced many people who were convinced they should rule. Constantine was raised in the Imperial Court. He encountered Christianity in the court circles as well. Fighting broke out among those who'd set their eyes on the throne. Constantine knew he could make a difference in the Roman Empire if he could defeat Maxentius.

Constantine didn't have the same number of soldiers as his opponent, but he felt he had God on his side. With his band of soldiers, he fought against Maxentius' first, second, and third armies. And then he turned his sights to Rome.

Constantine marched to Rome on October 28, 312, his confidence bolstered by a vision he'd had the previous night.

On the evening of October 27, far outnumbered, Constantine was promised victory in a dream. He was told that if the soldiers put Christ's monogram (initials) on their shields, they would defeat the enemy.

They neared the Milvian Bridge over the Tiber River. Constantine questioned if Maxentius would meet him in battle. Maxentius had organized the stockpiling of large amounts of food in case of an attack.[5] Yet Maxentius did withdraw from the city to meet up with Constantine. Their armies faced off.

Maxentius and his army made his stand in front of the Milvian Bridge. It was a stone bridge that crossed the Tiber River into Rome. Worried that Constantine's men would cross the bridge and take over the city, Maxentius partially destroyed the bridge. Then he had a pontoon (floating) bridge constructed to get his army back across the river.

When the two armies met, Constantine's army proved to be stronger. Maxentius' soldiers were also too close to the river to regroup. Maxentius tried to go back, but there was only one escape route—they had to cross the river. They started to escape, yet as the men tried to cross, their boats broke apart and the men disappeared into the water.

"They went into the depths like a stone," historians recorded[6]. And Constantine thought of Moses: "He cast Pharaoh's chariots and host into the sea, and overwhelmed his chosen charioteers in the Red Sea, and covered them with the flood."[7] The enemy soldiers still left on the shore were either captured or killed. Maxentius also died, drowning in the river while trying to escape.[8]

Constantine entered Rome on October 29. He sang to God, the ruler and victor, as he entered in triumph, and the people accepted him. The senate, the leaders, and the people received him as their leader.

And when a statue was crafted of him, Constantine put the sign of the cross in the statue's right hand, and ordered that this be inscribed: "By this salutary sign, the true proof of bravery, I have saved and freed your city from the yoke of the tyrant; and moreover, having set at liberty both the senate and the people of Rome, I have restored them to their ancient distinction and splendor."[9]

Constantine trusted that he followed God into battle, and humbled himself and his troops in prayer. Because of this, history was forever changed.

Little is much with God

When Constantine went into battle, there were an estimated 100,000 men in Maxentius' army against the 20,000 in Constantine's army.[10] When Constantine saw how his enemy was outnumbered, his mind went back to the Biblical story of the Red Sea opening for the Israelites. Both Moses and Constantine faced a mighty army, but both enemy armies sank into the depths of the water. "Sing to the LORD, for he is highly exalted. Both horse and driver he has hurled into the sea" (Exodus 15:21).

In both cases, the weaker group became the victor. When we turn to God in prayer, he is trustworthy. God can protect those who turn to him in their time of need. The impossible can become possible with God.

Something to Think About

Do you find it hard to pray about things that seem "too big?" What should you pray about anyway? How has God answered a big prayer of someone you know?

In His Own Words

When Constantine came into power, he made a lot of changes. He even wrote up this prayer, which he and his soldiers repeated together every Sunday morning:

We acknowledge Thee the only God. We own Thee as our King, and implore Thy succor. By Thy favor have we gotten the victory. Through Thee are we mightier than our enemies. We render thanks for Thy past benefits, and trust Thee for future blessings. Together we pray to Thee, and beseech Thee long to preserve to us, safe and triumphant, our emperor Constantine and his pious sons.[11]

That prayer uses words that aren't common today, but we can pray for God's favor and protection in our own way. We need to remember God and his work in our lives. We need to praise him for being bigger than our enemies. We need to ask for his guidance and protection in our lives. And we need to pray those things often. When we pray, we remember who is really in control. God is and always will be, no matter our place in history.

How He Changed History

Constantine was the first Roman emperor to say he had converted to Christianity. He helped publish the Edict of Milan, which declared acceptance of Christianity. He organized the First Council of Nicea in 325, at which the leaders of various churches came to together to arrange their beliefs in the Nicene Creed. Constantine's victory at the Milvian Bridge gave him total control of the western Roman Empire, paving the way for Christianity to become the main religion of the Roman Empire and ultimately of Europe.[12] Constantine's personal faith has been called into question by some historians. No one can deny that he helped bring about first the acceptance and then the embracing of Christianity by the Roman population.

it's in the Bible

Just like the story of Constantine, there are many biblical kings who asked their soldiers to pray for God's favor. Jehoshaphat was another one of them.

Three nations had come to make war on God's people. Jehoshaphat, the king, was afraid. He asked for all the people to come together to fast and pray.

> Some time later the Moabites and Ammonites, accompanied by Meunites, joined forces to make war on Jehoshaphat. Jehoshaphat received this intelligence report: "A huge force is on its way from beyond the Dead Sea to fight you. There's no time to waste—they're already at Hazazon Tamar, the oasis of En Gedi."

*Shaken, Jehoshaphat prayed. He went to GOD for
help and ordered a nationwide fast. The country of Judah
united in seeking GOD's help—they came from all the
cities of Judah to pray to GOD.*

*Then Jehoshaphat took a position before the assem-
bled people of Judah and Jerusalem at The Temple of GOD
in front of the new courtyard and said, "O GOD, God of
our ancestors, are you not God in heaven above and ruler
of all kingdoms below? You hold all power and might in
your fist—no one stands a chance against you!"*

—2 Chronicles 20:1–6 (MSG)

Jehoshaphat knew the power of his enemies. He also
knew where to turn for help—God.

*"O dear God, won't you take care of them? We're
helpless before this vandal horde ready to attack us. We
don't know what to do; we're looking to you." Everyone
in Judah was there—little children, wives, sons—all
present and attentive to GOD.*

—2 Chronicles 20:12–13 (MSG)

A prophet of God then told Jehoshaphat to not be
afraid—God was going to fight the battle for them. The
people were overjoyed.

*After talking it over with the people, Jehoshaphat ap-
pointed a choir for GOD; dressed in holy robes, they were
to march ahead of the troops, singing, Give thanks to
GOD, His love never quits.*

—2 Chronicles 20:21 (MSG)

The next day they went to battle, singing praises to
God. When the Israelites went into battle, all they saw

were dead bodies. The Lord had set ambushes against the men, and the armies had destroyed each other. Not only that, but when Jehoshaphat and all the people went to take the plunder, they couldn't carry it all. There was too much equipment, clothing, and valuables.

> *Jehoshaphat then led all the men of Judah and Jerusalem back to Jerusalem—an exuberant parade. GOD had given them joyful relief from their enemies! They entered Jerusalem and came to The Temple of GOD with all the instruments of the band playing.*
>
> *When the surrounding kingdoms got word that GOD had fought Israel's enemies, the fear of God descended on them. Jehoshaphat heard no more from them; as long as Jehoshaphat reigned, peace reigned.*
>
> *—2 Chronicles 20:27–30 (MSG)*

The people did their part ... they praised God. And God did his part ... defeating their enemies.

Your Life

In your life, there will be obstacles to get past. The bigger the problem looks, the more people you might want to have join you in prayer. Then, when God shows up in amazing ways, all those people will also get to rejoice with you in God's answered prayer. They will see God in ways they never saw him before. You will too!

God fights for his people when they gather together and seek his help.

CHAPTER 3

ST. PATRICK OF IRELAND

God Speaks Through Dreams

http://etc.usf.edu/clipart

When He Lived: ca. 387 – 461 AD[13]

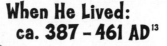

→ 432 AD

Patrick returns to Ireland

Patrick's eyes popped opened and he scanned the room, trying to remember where he was. The smallest amount of morning light filtered through the open window. His breath released, remembering that he was home. Home. For many years, Patrick had doubted he'd ever be home with his family again.

Patrick had grown up learning that the Roman Empire had once been a great empire, but when he was a boy, that wasn't the case. Various peoples had flooded across Roman borders, bringing with them new languages and new problems. The nation was in debt, and many depended on money from the government to live.

Patrick grew up with his parents on the coast of Britain in the town of Bonavern, Taberniae.[14] His father was a magistrate and a deacon in their church. His grandfather was a minister. Patrick himself was not interested in religion and was practically an atheist as a teenager. (If someone is an atheist, it means they do not believe in God.)

Patrick was only sixteen when his worst nightmare came true. He was kidnapped by raiders and sold as a slave in Ireland. Ireland was a very different place than Britain. The people there believed in very different things, including dark forces. Patrick had grown up with a family who believed in God and who made the Lord the center of their lives. The people in Ireland — the Druids — had ungodly ways.

As a slave in Ireland, Patrick herded pigs. He learned the people's language and saw how the Druids and pagans cast magic spells, believed in superstitions, and committed human sacrifice. There was little that Patrick could do for them, but he remembered the faith of his family and he began to pray. The more he prayed, the more he understood God's Spirit within him. It was the Spirit who led Patrick to escape to the coast.[15] On the seacoast, Patrick found a ship that carried him to freedom. Or so Patrick thought. Leaving the coast of Ireland behind him, Patrick was free, but it wasn't easy to get home.

Soon after Patrick boarded the ship, a storm blew in. The ship was carried to Gaul (France). In Gaul, Patrick spent a few months in a monastery on the island of St. Honorat.[16]

Eventually, Patrick made it home, but he did not leave behind the memory of the people of Ireland. He continued to think about their great need for God. Patrick prayed for the people. Then one night, a dream came—one he never forgot.

> I saw a man coming, as it were from Ireland. His name was Victorius, and he carried many letters, and he gave me one of them. I read the heading: "The Voice of the Irish." As I began the letter, I imagined in that moment that I heard the voice of those very people who were near the wood of Foclut, which is beside the western sea—and they cried out, as with one voice: "We appeal to you, holy servant boy, to come and walk among us."[17]

In his dream, the people wanted to know about God, and they knew that Patrick was the one who could share the Good News with them.

Patrick awoke, and pain was tight in his chest. How would those in Ireland know the truth of Christ unless someone shared it with them? Was this a message from God? Did God want him to return to the place of his captivity?

Patrick left his family once again—this time by choice. He went to Europe and trained for the ministry. Then, in 432, when he was 40 years old, Patrick returned to Ireland. He did not go alone. Through the years, many monks journeyed with him. We know about Patrick's story because he wrote it in his own words in a book called *Confession*.

Patrick spent the next thirty years telling hundreds of

people about Jesus. Many miracles that Patrick performed, through the strength of God, are recorded. His life was not easy. Patrick lived in poverty for years, traveled often, and suffered greatly to teach those who were following evil how to follow God. Yet because of St. Patrick's prayers—and his willingness to return to share the good news of Jesus in Ireland—history was forever changed.

We don't have to be great to be used by God, just willing

Patrick was an ordinary person when God called him to return to Ireland. He rose up and became a missionary and bishop, but all of that started with a "yes."

"For I command you today to love the Lord your God, to walk in obedience to him, and to keep his commands, decrees and laws; then you will live and increase, and the Lord your God will bless you in the land you are entering to possess" (Deuteronomy 30:16).

Not only did God call Patrick to share the good news of Jesus, but God also called him to return to a place where many evil practices were commonplace. Since Patrick was taken to Ireland as a captive, he probably didn't ever want to return, yet he did, and thousands and thousands of lives were changed.

St. Patrick is the best-known saint connected with Ireland. Today we even celebrate St. Patrick's Day to honor his works and the Irish heritage. In some parts of the world, St. Patrick's Day is a celebration of all things Irish, but in Ireland it is a day of religious observance to celebrate St. Patrick's works on the day of his death.

Have you ever wondered why we decorate with shamrocks (three-leaf clovers) on St. Patrick's Day? The legend is that Patrick used the shamrock to explain the Trinity, and this image has been associated with him and the Irish people since that time.[18]

Something to Think About

Patrick was an ordinary boy who ended up being far from home. How does God sometimes use the hard stuff in life to change us? What would have happened if Patrick had said to God, "No, I don't want to return to Ireland"?

God is probably not sending you to somewhere foreign at this time, but where can you share the good news of Jesus? For whom can you pray?

In His Own Words

The Lord opened the understanding of my unbelief, that, last as it was, I might remember my faults and turn to the Lord my God with all my heart, and he had regard to my low estate, and pitied my youth and ignorance, and kept guard over me even before I knew Him.[19]

How He Changed History

Though it is sometimes hard to separate fact from fiction in the stories of St. Patrick, it is certain that Patrick was one of the first great Christian missionaries. He established many churches in Ireland. The towns where Christian churches were established became the first cities in Ireland. They also became centers of art, learning, and culture. Patrick's example also inspired many Celtic monks to spread the gospel in Scotland, England, and Europe. In addition to that, Patrick's strong stand against slavery in Ireland eventually ended the Irish slave trade. We'll also never know the number of lives who were changed as they turned away from evil practices and discovered faith in the one true God.

it's in the Bible

St. Patrick wasn't the only one who was called to take the Good News of Jesus to a pagan nation through a dream. The Apostle Paul had a similar dream, which is recounted in Acts 16:9–10.

Paul and his companions were traveling, preaching the Word of God. One night, Paul had a vision about a man from Macedonia. The man asked Paul to come and speak to the people there. Paul believed it was a message from God and traveled there, spreading the Good News.

> That night Paul had a dream: A Macedonian stood on the far shore and called across the sea, "Come over to Macedonia and help us!" The dream gave Paul his map. We went to work at once getting things ready to cross over to Macedonia. All the pieces had come together. We knew now for sure that God had called us to preach the good news to the Europeans.   —Acts 16:9–10 (MSG)

God wants people from all over the world to know about him. Like Saint Patrick and Paul show us, it takes our obedience to make that happen. In order for people to know about Jesus, someone needs to tell them. Sometimes this means traveling to a new place. Other times it means telling a friend or a neighbor about Jesus. But when we are willing to obey, we never know how history will be changed.

Your Life

God might not send a message to you in a dream, but maybe he will. Each of us needs to prepare ourselves to tell others about God. We do this by seeking him, praying to him, and studying his Word. When we prepare our minds and hearts, we can share what we learn with others.

Willingness to follow God and obedience are important, but remember that we aren't left on our own. God is with us always. He'll give us the words we need to say when we need them. He doesn't give us a job and send us off alone to do it. Because Jesus is in our hearts, he is with us wherever we go.

Sometimes God speaks to us in unusual ways, and he is with us as we obey.

CHAPTER 4

OSWALD, KING OF NORTHUMBRIA

God's Army Will Fight for Those Who Believe

When He Lived: ca. 604 – 642 AD

→ **633 AD**

Oswald returns to reclaim his country

Oswald was only 11 years old when his father died. Oswald's father was king of Northumbria (present-day parts of England and Scotland), and Oswald knew he was next in line to be king. He also knew he wasn't prepared.

When Oswald's father died after a military defeat, his uncle Edwin became king. Fearing for her sons' lives, Aacha, Oswald's mother, took their family to Scotland. It was here the family converted to Christianity and Oswald was sent to a monastery for his education. He was filled with uncertainty as he left the home he'd always known, but Oswald found refuge with Columba's monks on the isle of Iona. (A monk is a special person who has set himself aside to live for God. Monks do not marry. They are men who live in a small community, and they care for each other and for those who God brings them.) These monks told Oswald about Jesus.

The monks explained what it means to accept Jesus as Lord. Oswald learned that there was a king even greater than the kings on the earth. Oswald's father had been the king of a small country, but the monks taught Oswald that there was a heavenly king who will never leave us, and that is Jesus Christ.

Oswald grew up at the monastery, and it was easy to follow Jesus there. The monks encouraged him, and they often met for Bible reading and prayer. But when Oswald became an adult, he knew it would soon be time to go. He would have to leave the safety of the monastery and return to Northumbria to take over the kingdom that his father had ruled. But to do that, there would be conflict on the battlefield first.[20]

In 633 AD King Edwin of Northumbria was killed in a battle against Penda and Cadwallon. Oswald was 29 years old, and he knew it was his time to step up and succeed King Edwin on the throne.

Oswald assembled an army to fight against those who'd overtaken Northumbria. He didn't have much of a fighting force. And out of all his men, only a few knew Jesus Christ. Yet Oswald's heart was full of faith. The lessons from God's Word that he'd learned from the monks were with him.

The men had been assembled, and Oswald strode around them. He knew it was only God who would win the battle for them. He wanted the men to understand this too.

The night before battle, Oswald set up a large cross. He gripped the wood upright while a few of his men packed dirt into the hole around the wooden cross. All of his soldiers looked at him curiously, and Oswald lifted his voice, "Let us now kneel down and together pray to the Almighty and only true God that he will mercifully defend us from our enemy; for he knows that we fight in defense of our lives and country."[21]

Oswald and his men prayed together. For many of these men, it was the first time they had ever prayed. They most likely had many questions about why Oswald would serve a god he could not see. They probably also wondered if God would be with them as Oswald declared God would.

That night, as Oswald rested, he had a vision. In the vision he was assured that he would have victory. The next day, it was proven that God was indeed with that army. Even though they were greatly outnumbered, Oswald's men were victorious.

Most importantly, the soldiers saw that Oswald's prayers were answered. Many soldiers decided to put their faith in this God that they could not see, and these soldiers became followers of Jesus Christ.

Oswald was later killed in the Battle of Maserfield. He died after praying that God would protect the soldiers, but sadly they too died. He was a brave king who not only led his people in battle, but also led them to Christ. While Oswald was able to convert many, pagans were still in

England. Those who followed behind him would be able to build on his works, and history was forever changed.

It's our job to tell others about Jesus

Oswald prayed that God would lead his troops to victory. Oswald took the knowledge that he had about God and shared it with the soldiers under his command. He dared to believe that God was on his side. He listened to God's voice—God's message of victory—and shared it with his troops. Because Oswald was willing to tell his soldiers about Jesus, they understood that the victory wasn't in their own strength. The following Scripture passage was written down over 500 years before Oswald lived, yet Oswald understood that for his troops to know about God he had to tell them.

> That is why the Holy Spirit says, "Today when you hear his voice, don't harden your hearts as Israel did when they rebelled, when they tested me in the wilderness. There your ancestors tested and tried my patience, even though they saw my miracles for forty years. So I was angry with them, and I said, 'Their hearts always turn away from me. They refuse to do what I tell them.' So in my anger I took an oath: 'They will never enter my place of rest.' "
>
> Be careful then, dear brothers and sisters. Make sure that your own hearts are not evil and unbelieving, turning you away from the living God. You must warn each other every day, while it is still "today," so that none of you will be deceived by sin and hardened against God. For if we are faithful to the end, trusting God just as firmly as when we first believed, we will share in all that belongs to Christ.   —Hebrews 3:7–14 (NLT)

Everywhere we go there are people who don't under-stand that Jesus is there for us, in the good times and the hard times. It's our job to tell others about God. Like Oswald, we can show that our God is with us, fighting for us.

Something to Think About

As a young man, Oswald was in a safe place in the monastery. Why do you think it was important for Oswald to return to his people rather than staying in the safety and peacefulness of the monastery? How can you inspire others—by telling them about the living God—while it is still today?

In His Own Words

Sometimes the most important thing isn't what we have to say. Instead, it's what others have to say about us. One historian who lived long ago, named Bede, had this to say about Oswald. He wrote it less than a century after Oswald's death:

From that time, as the days went by, many came from the country of the Irish into Britain and to those English kingdoms over which Oswald reigned, preaching the word of faith with great devotion. Those of them who held the rank of priest administered the grace of baptism to those who believed. Churches were built in various places and the people flocked together with joy to hear the

> Word; lands and property of other kinds were given by royal bounty to establish monasteries, and English children, as well as their elders, were instructed by Irish teachers in advanced studies and in the observance of the disciple of a Rule.[22]

How He Changed History

After their victory in battle, Oswald restored order throughout Northumbria. He also asked missionaries from Scotland to come and teach the people of his country about Jesus. One of the missionaries was Aidan.[23] Oswald became Aidan's translator so that he could help the people hear and understand the Bible. The people started churches all over Northumbria. Thousands of people in his country became Christians.[24] Oswald also married Kineburga, the Princess of Wessex. She and her father, the King of Wessex, converted to Christianity. This allowed the religion to spread into southwestern England. Wessex would later become the most powerful part of England, which would encourage Christianity to continue to spread even farther.

it's in the Bible

In the Bible, there was another young man who became king and who faced many battles with God's help. In 2 Samuel 5:17–25, we hear about a young man named David. When he was crowned king of Israel, the countries nearby were not happy. In fact, the Philistines were so mad that they decided to hunt for him to kill him. The Philistines came and deployed their forces in Raphaim Valley.

> Then David prayed to GOD: "Shall I go up and fight the Philistines? Will you help me beat them?"
>
> "Go up," GOD replied. "Count on me. I'll help you beat them."
>
> David then went straight to Baal Perazim, and smashed them to pieces. Afterward David said, "GOD exploded on my enemies like a gush of water." That's why David named the place Baal Perazim (The-Master-Who-Explodes). The retreating Philistines dumped their idols, and David and his soldiers took them away.
>
> Later there was a repeat performance. The Philistines came up again and deployed their troops in the Rephaim Valley. David again prayed to GOD.
>
> This time God said, "Don't attack them head-on. Instead, circle around behind them and ambush them from the grove of sacred trees. When you hear the sound of shuffling in the trees, get ready to move out. It's a signal that GOD is going ahead of you to smash the Philistine camp."
>
> David did exactly what GOD told him. He routed the Philistines all the way from Gibeon to Gezer."
>
> —2 Samuel 5:19–25 (MSG)

What a victory! Can you imagine what it was like to hear the sound of God's army shuffling in the trees? It must have been amazing. God proved to David that he was someone who could be counted on. God helped David beat his enemies. God proved that he was most powerful of all.

Your Life

In your life you most likely won't face enemies on the battlefield like Oswald of Northumbria or like King David from the Bible, but you will have your own battles. Your battles might be with bullies at school who don't treat others well. Or you may battle against fears such as fear of a test, fear of moving to a new town, or fear of telling another person about Jesus. No matter what you fear, God will always be there for you. God wants you to turn to him in prayer.

Sometimes we may feel as if God gets tired of hearing our prayers. He doesn't. Instead he says, "Count on me. I'll help you beat this." God wants you to turn to him. When you do, your faith is strengthened. Also, when you turn to him, other people see that God is available to help us in our times of need.

You'll never know how your answered prayers will cause other people to believe in Jesus. All of us, even strong men and women, boys and girls, need to bow down and ask God for help. And God will always be there to help you.

Strong men also need to bow down in order to show others that it is God who brings the victory.

CHAPTER 5

CHRISTOPHER COLUMBUS

Prayer Reminds Us to Keep Going

When He Lived:
ca. 1451 – 1506 AD

→ 1492 AD

Christopher's trust in God leads him to a new world

Christopher Columbus's fingers tightened around the ship's rail. He closed his eyes and lifted his face toward the sun. Golden rays warmed his cheeks. He smiled as he listened to the wind in the sails. There was nothing better than an ocean voyage, especially one that he had dreamed about for so many years.

Christopher opened his eyes. Sailors scurried on the deck like worker ants. He nodded his approval. Each time the sailors expertly set the sails or battled difficult waves, they brought Christopher closer to land.

October 10, 1492 had dawned as a beautiful morning.

But a few minutes later, the sun didn't seem nearly as warm, or the blue ocean as thrilling, when one of Christopher's two companion ships pulled alongside the Santa María.

"Martín and Vicente Pinzón demand a meeting!" a sailor called.

Christopher signaled the two captains to board.

The men seemed pleasant enough upon their boarding, but their true feelings were revealed when they entered Christopher's stateroom—a private area for the admiral of the sea.

"We must turn back." Martín's worried eyes fixed on Christopher. "We have been at sea thirty-one days. We have gone too far—farther than you'll even admit."

Vicente continued in the same uneasy tone as his brother. "It is foolishness to keep sailing westward with no sign of land. We will all perish. Our crews have threatened to throw us overboard if we do not turn back."

Christopher's stomach knotted like the ropes above him. He understood their fear. None of them had ever been more than three hundred miles at sea. Now they were well over three thousand and still going.

He stared out of his stateroom porthole. Each wave the ship pushed through reminded him of the obstacles he had faced over the last eight years. Only by God's grace had he kept going. This was his chance. His only chance. Still, what good was his dream without a crew backing him up?

Christopher turned from the window and faced Martín and Vicente. "Yes, we'll turn back, but on one condition."

The men waited for him to continue.

"Promise me today and two more days," Christopher

said somberly. "If we do not sight land by October 12, we'll head for home."[25]

Later when he was alone, Christopher replayed the conversation in his mind.

"Three more days," he whispered to himself. *Am I some kind of fool? What if land is four days away, or five?*

Faith glimmered like a single candle in his heart.

The three ships were getting close to land. Christopher knew it. A few mornings ago, as he had stood in his favorite spot, he'd seen a flock of birds in the distance. Small birds, land birds, flying southwest.

"Land has to be that direction," he had told his pilot. "Adjust our course to follow them."

Despite the crew's growing doubt, Christopher desired to press onward. Hadn't God given him this idea in the first place? Would a loving God take him this far for nothing?

Christopher rubbed his weary eyes, then knelt in his cabin. The masts groaned above him. The ship swayed beneath. Men's voices echoed through the walls. Only three more days. The thought was more than he could bear.

And so Christopher prayed. He prayed to God who had created the ocean—God who had created the land he had sailed from ... and the land he was sailing to. He prayed for swift winds in their sails, and signs to give them hope. He prayed that the men's hearts be lifted. He prayed like never before, for Christopher needed a miracle.

The next morning, the sunlight beamed down on Christopher, warming his shoulders, his heart. White, fluffy clouds dotted the horizon. Salty water sprayed off the hull, leaving a cool mist in the air.

It was a good day to find land. But the hours passed and

nothing changed. The expanse of ocean stretched before him with no sign of land. Had God not heard his prayers?

Finally, one of the sailors saw something — fresh weeds, like the kind found in rivers, floated past. Later, a branch with rose berries bobbed in the waves. Most importantly, a carved stick was pulled from the water. Grooves and marks in the wood proved it had been shaped with an iron tool. The sailors watched diligently. Their voices took on a happier note as they called to each other and sang.

That night, Christopher spoke to his men. "God is good," he told those gathered around him. "He has given us a gentle ocean and new signs to lift our spirits. He has given us good winds, better than ever! Yesterday, we covered fifty-nine leagues — our second best time. Today, we saw new signs of land." His voice rose with excitement. "God is leading us to the Promised Land!"

After Christopher's speech, everyone stayed on deck. Not one eye closed that night. Christopher positioned himself at high stern (the back of the ship). All was quiet until 10 o'clock. Then, Christopher spotted what he had been looking for. A light!

He called to one of the royal Spanish advisors. "Do you see it, the light in the distance? It's like a wax candle being raised and lowered."

"Aye, admiral," the man responded. "I do." A second man was called, but by the time he arrived, the light had disappeared. Christopher notified the crew, but most of them shrugged off the significance. Still, Christopher had no doubt. God was answering his prayers.

Then, at two in the morning, with less than four hours remaining before the dawn of the third day, cannon fire from the lead ship gave the joyful signal that land was spotted.

"Land!" the sailors shouted. Laughter filled the air. One sailor grabbed the arm of another and they did a jig. Like a flame moving through a dry field, the dancing spread with vigor as they rejoiced.

"Land," Christopher whispered. His heart leapt like the feet of those around him. He lifted his face toward the heavens. A smile touched his lips.

Later that morning, Christopher was the first to set foot on the white coral beach. He named the land San Salvador—Holy Savior. His eyes filled with tears as he knelt.

"Holy Savior," he prayed, "O Lord, Almighty and everlasting God, by Thy holy Word thou has created the heaven, and the earth, and the sea; blessed and glorified by Thy Name, and praised be Thy Majesty, which hath designed to use us, Thy humble servants, that Thy holy Name may be proclaimed in this second part of earth."[26]

Christopher Columbus had discovered a land previously unknown to most of the world. A place no European had been to before. (This land was later named Hispaniola and is now the modern-day countries of Haiti and the Dominican Republic.)

Christopher's prayers were answered. He had found a second part of the earth on October 12, 1492, and history was forever changed.

Press on

Philippians 3:14 says, "I press on toward the goal to win the prize for which God has called me heavenward in Christ Jesus."

In life our ultimate calling is to press on toward heaven, but God will also call individuals, as he did Christopher Columbus to set sail in new directions.

Where did Columbus get the idea to sail west? Was he an educated man who wanted to prove a theory? No, in his book *Libro de las profecias* (Book of Prophecies), Columbus wrote:

It was the Lord who put into my mind (I could feel His hand upon me) the fact that it would be possible to sail from here to the Indies. All who heard of my project rejected it with laughter, ridiculing me.

There was no question that the inspiration was from the Holy Spirit, because he comforted me with rays of marvelous illumination for the Holy Scriptures ... encouraging me continually to press forward, and without ceasing for a moment they now encourage me to make haste.[27]

Something to Think About

What was Christopher Columbus's reason for voyaging across the vast ocean? What did he wish to find in the West Indies? Riches? Power or fame? To share his faith?

Below is a journal entry that Columbus wrote for Queen Isabella of Spain. Sadly, once Columbus got to the new world, his desire for gold became even more important than faith. This is a reminder to all of us to keep our eyes focused on God first ... and most.

> Therefore, your highnesses determined to send me, Christopher Columbus, to the said parts of India, to see the said prince, and the people and lands, and discover the nature and disposition of them all, and the means to be taken for the conversions of them to our holy faith; and ordered that I should not go by land to the east, by which it is the custom to go, but by a voyage to the west, by which of course, unto the present time, we do not know for certain that anyone hath passed.[28]

In His Own Words

From the Admiral's Log

> Thursday, 11 October. Steered west-southwest; and encountered a heavier sea than they had met with before in the whole voyage. Saw pardelas and a green rush {stiff marsh plants} near the vessel. The crew of the Pinta saw a cane and a log; they also picked up a stick which appeared to have been carved with an iron tool, a piece of cane, a plant which grows on land, and a board. The crew of the Niña saw other signs of land, and a stalk loaded with rose berries. These signs encouraged them, and they all grew cheerful. Sailed this day till sunset, twenty-seven leagues.

> After sunset steered their original course west and sailed twelve miles an hour till two hours after midnight, going ninety miles, which are twenty-two leagues and a half; and as the Pinta was the swiftest sailor, and kept ahead of the Admiral, she discovered land and made the signals which had been ordered.[29]

How He Changed History

In many ways, explorers who traveled to America did good by bringing knowledge, such as farming practices. They also brought horses, which allowed Native Americans to expand their hunting practices. However, though Columbus and other explorers may have had good intentions at first, they were sinful people, just as we all are. They often brought violence and disease with them. They took advantage of native people.

This is why it is always important to remember Paul's words to the Philippians: "Let each of you look not only to his own interests, but also to the interests of others" (Philippians 2:4 ESV) and the words of Christ: "My command is this: Love each other as I have loved you" (John 15:12).

it's in the Bible

From ancient times Christians have prayed in many different ways. Kneeling is one way. Christopher Columbus was known to pray this way. The Bible tells about many people who knelt in prayer, such as the leper in Mark 1:40.

> *A leper came to him, begging on his knees, "If you want to, you can cleanse me." Deeply moved, Jesus put out his hand, touched him, and said, "I want to. Be clean." Then and there the leprosy was gone, his skin smooth and healthy."*   —*Mark 1:40–41 (MSG)*

Another way to pray is with your arms lifted with your palms open. This prayer position is called orans. The word *orans* comes from the Latin for "prayer." During Jesus' time, this was a common way to pray. Jesus prayed this way on many occasions. The most important thing is not how we pray, but that we do pray.

Your Life

God always hears us, whether we're kneeling, sitting, or standing on our heads. Yet, just as kneeling before a king is a sign of respect, when we kneel in prayer, we are showing honor to God, our King. When we humble ourselves, God will hear our prayer.

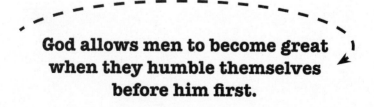

God allows men to become great when they humble themselves before him first.

CHAPTER 6

MARTIN LUTHER

Praying to Stand Firm

When He Lived: 1483 – 1546 AD

→ 1521 AD

Martin Luther defends his work

Martin Luther climbed into the horse-drawn wagon and scanned his friends' faces.

A woman grasped Martin's hand. "I've heard church supporters plan to burn you at the stake. Please stay here in Wittenberg."

Martin shook his head. "They can burn me at the stake, if that's what they choose, but I will not take back my teachings. I'll stand firm on this one fact—God's forgiveness is for everyone, free for the asking. Just as the Scriptures read."

He adjusted his simple black robe and settled in for the journey. "Besides, friends, just imagine. I'll be speaking face to face with bishops. I'll be able to discuss the Bible with the emperor himself. Perhaps our prayers will be answered, and all men, not just church leaders, will be able to read God's Word for themselves."

It was the Tuesday before Easter, 1521. Martin had been called to face church leaders. The leaders taught that God's forgiveness must be bought. Martin had attended school and he knew how to read Latin, the language of the Bible. A coal miner's son, Martin had dedicated himself as a monk and studied the Scriptures. Through studying the Bible, Martin learned that people are not saved by their works or deeds. Instead, they are saved through Jesus Christ when they have faith in him. Martin also believed that God required no money or goods in order to forgive, as church leaders were teaching at that time. Martin spread this message to normal people, commoners, through speeches and books he'd written. He also translated the Bible into German so everyday people could read it, not just those who knew Latin.

In the city of Worms, Martin was brought before the council.

A burly official neared Martin and waved his hands toward a pile of books. "First, are you willing to confess you have written these books? Second, are you ready to renounce them? Will you say that you will no longer stick by these words?"

"May I have time to consider my answer?" Martin asked with respect. He didn't want to answer on the fly. Instead, Martin wanted time to think, and pray, about what he was going to say.

The court officials seemed surprised Martin didn't immediately defend himself. Whispers erupted around the room.

"Tomorrow," the man said. "You have until tomorrow."

The next day, Martin stood in front of the same sneering faces.

"To answer your question," Martin said humbly and gently, "I have to say that all my books are not the same. Some are books of prayer. Others were written against the enemies of the gospel. I realize I am human. I realize I could have made mistakes. Maybe I have criticized other men too harshly. So please show me in the Bible where any of my books are wrong, and I'll be the first to throw my words into the fire."

The court official raised his voice. "Give us a short, clear answer."

Luther prayed for wisdom … aloud. "Since your Majesty and your Lordships ask for a simple reply, I will give you one without horns or teeth. Unless I am proved to be wrong by the testimony of Scriptures and by plain reasoning … I am bound in conscience and hold fast to the Word of God. I cannot and I will not retract anything, for it is neither safe nor right to act against one's conscience. God help me! Amen."[30]

"A heretic! A heretic!" the men in the room hissed. "Questioner of the church. He will not take back his words or his writings. Take him to the fire."

But because Martin had important friends, the emperor let him go. Still, danger threatened Martin. He had been labeled a heretic and a questioner of the church. This meant that if someone murdered Martin, that man would not be punished.

After his release, Martin's friends hid him. But Martin could not stay out of sight for long. Instead, he worked day and night to translate the New Testament into German. He also traveled the countryside speaking and teaching God's Word. And history was forever changed.

Faith comes by hearing

Do you own a Bible? If you do then you are benefitting from the hard work of others. People have worked for hundreds of years to make God's Word available to people like you and me all around the world.

Romans 10:17 says, "So faith comes from hearing, that is, hearing the Good News about Christ" (NLT). Martin Luther knew that it was important for the people to be able to read God's Word for themselves. Because of Martin Luther's work, ordinary people are able to read the Bible for themselves and believe in our Lord.

Something to Think About

There are people all around the world who don't have a Bible of their own. There are probably even people in your neighborhood who don't own a Bible or have never read one. Is it easy or hard for people to learn about God if they don't have a Bible? Is there someone you can thank for teaching God's Word to you? Who?

In His Own Words

In addition to translating the Bible and writing many books, Martin Luther also wrote many hymns. You may even sing in your church hymns that he wrote.

> A mighty fortress is our God,
> A bulwark never failing...
> Let goods and kindred go,
> This mortal life also;
> The body they may kill:
> God's truth abideth still
> His kingdom is forever.[31]

Some of those words may be hard to understand, but what is the message of the song?

How He Changed History

Martin Luther is one of the fathers of the Protestant Reformation. It was a time when many changes happened in the church to make the knowledge of God accessible to ordinary people. Martin Luther made people think differently about the way they'd always done things. His translation of the Bible into common German allowed everyday German citizens to read God's Word for themselves. This impacted the German culture and language of his day. Martin Luther's translation of the Bible also influenced the creation of the English Tyndale Bible. This allowed God's Word to spread to England, too. And God's Word could impact people's hearts in a whole new way.

it's in the Bible

Martin Luther's story is similar to a biblical story in Acts 4:5–20. The religious leaders in Jerusalem brought Peter and John before them. The religious leaders had seen a man healed "in the name of Jesus," and they didn't want the news to spread. If the people believed in Jesus, they would stop following the rules that the religious leaders gave them.

> Then they called them in again and commanded them not to speak or teach at all in the name of Jesus. But Peter and John replied, "Which is right in God's eyes: to listen to you, or to him? You be the judges! As for us, we cannot help speaking about what we have seen and heard." After further threats they let them go. They could not decide how to punish them, because all the people were praising God for what had happened.   —Acts 4:18–21

The religious leaders threatened Peter and John, but after the two disciples were released, they continued to share the good news of Jesus with boldness—just like Martin Luther. People heard the good news, and it spread.

Your Life

Every day we face choices of whether to talk about our God or try to pretend we don't know him. When have you been tempted to back down to peer pressure? Was there a time when you were too embarrassed to pray? Maybe there was a time when you heard someone speaking badly about Christians? Or perhaps you ignored the opportunity to share the Good News of Jesus with a friend.

People may want to stop us from sharing God's Word, but we can pray for strength and courage. When Martin Luther faced the world's accusations, he cried for help and refused to keep silent. Peter and John did the same.

God loves to provide boldness through his Holy Spirit. This power isn't just for people who lived long ago. God can give you courage and help you to stand firm. Won't you turn to him? People come to faith when they hear God's Word, but they only get to hear it when someone brings it to them.

When we pray, God's power gives us the strength to stand strong and share the Good News of Jesus with others.

CHAPTER 7

GOVERNOR WILLIAM BRADFORD

God Answers Prayers in Amazing Ways

When He Lived: 1590 – 1657 AD

→ **1623 AD**

Governor William Bradford calls a fast, asking the Pilgrims to pray for rain to save their crops

William Bradford had so much hope when he and the other healthy colonists planted seeds in the ground. A congregation of Separatists, they'd come to the New World to gain religious freedom, yet their desire to serve God with a pure religion had cost them greatly.

Their group had arrived in New England in the winter of 1621, and nearly half of them—men, women, and children — had died. The following year had been better. With the help from the Native Americans, including Massasoit and others, they'd produced a harvest. They had celebrated together that fall. It was a time of thanksgiving for their new friends and for God's provision.

Yet by 1623, William worried that it would be another hard winter. Would he lose even more of his friends? The crops the colonists had so faithfully planted in spring were now dying because of lack of water. If it didn't rain soon, the crops would fail. No crops would mean they'd face the harsh New England winters without food, and William feared that would be the end of their small colony.

He knelt on the ground and picked up a handful of dirt, allowing it to filter through his fingers. The ground was dry, and the small stalks of corn were already starting to wither.

Heaviness weighed down on William's chest. He was only 33 years old, and his responsibility to the colony burdened him. Without good crops, he doubted any of his people could make it another year.

Lord, haven't we endured enough already?

William stood and sighed. He scanned the cloudless sky. He never could have claimed an easy life. Although he was born into what was considered a family of wealth and influence, the death of beloved family members had changed everything. William's father had died when William was just one year old. When he was four, his mother married a new husband, and young William was sent to live with his grandfather. Two years later, his grandfather died, and William returned to his mother. Sadly, she passed away shortly thereafter, and William became an orphan.[32]

More tragedy came when William became sick himself.

As an older boy he was unable to work or play, and he spent most of his time reading. While this was hard, this time became a key season in his life. William read the Bible and other important books. Knowing God's Word built a foundation of faith for the rest of his life.

As a teen, William became involved with Christian believers who wanted a more pure Christian Church. They weren't happy with the Church of England, especially the church's ties with Catholic practices.

In 1603, when King James I started dealing harshly with church critics, the group decided it would be impossible to reform the church. They decided to break things off with the church instead. They became known as Separatists because they wanted to separate themselves from the church. At 18 years old, William escaped England with the small congregation. They moved to the Dutch Republic (part of the Netherlands).

Some of the Separatists remained in the Dutch Republic, and others returned to London for a time, but all had one thing on their mind … by 1617 they had decided to set up a colony in the Americas. They had religious freedom in the Dutch Republic, but the congregation was disturbed by what they saw as the ungodly influence of some of the Dutch on their children.

A group of one hundred and two passengers and thirty crewmen left Plymouth, England on September 6, 1620. It was a hard voyage. Two people died at sea. Things were no easier when they made it to New England. In just a few months' time, nearly half of the passengers had died because of the harsh winter.

The following year was filled with further misfortunes

for the colonists. More ships had brought more people and no supplies. And now they faced a drought.

William's friend, Captain Miles Standish, had also worried about their fate. Captain Standish had taken a voyage in hopes of finding food and provisions. Yet they hadn't heard from the man. William knew the many dangers that awaited him. More than that, William knew it was God's help they needed most.

William let another handful of dirt slip through his fingers, and then he rose. The fields of corn stalks shriveled before him. The people couldn't take much more of this. If rain didn't come, all would be lost.

A Scripture verse that he'd read as a boy filtered through his mind, "If my people, which are called by my name, shall humble themselves, and pray, and seek my face, and turn from their wicked ways; then will I hear from heaven, and will forgive their sin, and will heal their land" (2 Chronicles 7:14 KJV).

William and the other colonists had worked so hard to build a new life, and now God was asking to be invited back in. It was only with the help of God that they could prosper in this new world.

In July, a day was appointed for fasting and prayer. The people gathered, knowing that God alone could save them. William watched the sky, not in fear, but in faith. Surely God would show up.

Nine hours later, clouds spread over the sky. William's heartbeat quickened and joy flooded his heart as a gentle rain fell. The corn stalks stood a little taller, revived by the much-needed rain.

And then something else wonderful happened ... Miles

returned. He brought food, but he also brought news. A ship was coming!

Thankfulness flooded William's heart. He thought back to the first fall harvest when the colonists had gathered with the Native Americans to thank God for his provision. William knew that God deserved all the glory again. As governor, William called a public service of thanksgiving and prayer.[33]

In July of 1623, the small group of colonists gathered for prayer and praise. Within days, the ship the *Anne* docked. Friends emerged from the hold, bringing provisions for the pilgrims. The new colonists were encouraged in their faith in God, and they grew stronger in spirit and in body.

The settlement grew and grew, and was the foundation for the United States of America. The colonists started as a small, needy group, yet they knew turning to God would make all the difference. Their humility and prayer brought rain, saving their crops and strengthening them. And history was forever changed.

When we trust in God, we are not disappointed

Governor William Bradford had faced a difficult illness as a child, but his time in bed allowed him to read God's Word. When we know God's Word, then we know God. We learn to trust him when we hear about his deeds.

Psalm 22:4–5 says, "Our ancestors trusted you. They trusted, and you rescued them. They cried to you and were saved. They trusted you and were never disappointed" (God's Word).

Just like our biblical forefathers trusted in God, so did others who came after them. The first colonists faced many hard things, but when they turned to God in prayer, he showed up in wonderful ways.

Something to Think About

Why does God sometimes allow difficult things, like a drought, to happen? What challenges have you faced in your life? When you turn to God in prayer, what things have changed inside you? How has prayer made a difference?

In His Own Words

Here are William's own words about the trust he and the other colonists put in God:

Upon which they set apart a solemn day of humiliation, to seek the Lord by humble and fervent prayer, in this great distress. And He was pleased to give them a gracious and speedy answer, both to their own and the Indians admiration that lived among them. For all the morning, and the greatest part of the day, it was clear weather and very hot and not a cloud or any sign of rain to be seen, yet toward evening it began to overcast, and shortly after to rain, with such sweet and gentle showers, and gave them cause of rejoicing, and blessing God.

It came without either wind, or thunder, or any violence, and by degrees in abundance, as that the earth was thoroughly wet and soaked therewith. Which did so apparently revive and quicken the decayed corn and other fruits, as was wonderful

> to see, and made the Indians astonished to behold, and afterwards the Lord sent them such seasonable showers with interchange of fair, warmer weather, as, through His blessing, caused a fruitful and liberal harvest, to their no small comfort and rejoicing. For which mercy, (in time convenient) they also set apart a day of thanksgiving.[34]
>
> *William Bradford*

Isn't it wonderful that the answer to prayer also astonished the Native Americans? When we have faith in God we get to experience his answers in amazing ways, and sometimes others do too.

And not only did the Native Americans get to experience it, but William also recounted the story of this answered prayer in his historical book, *Of Plymouth Plantation*. For hundreds of years, many readers have also learned of God's faithfulness.

How He Changed History

Under William Bradford's leadership, the Plymouth colony was one of few colonies to survive harsh conditions. This colony had no deserters and they were able to live in relative harmony with the Native Americans. The success of these new colonies would set the standard for the colonization of North America.

Would the Pilgrims have survived without the break in the drought that provided them with food? We can never know for sure. Would the drought have been broken without the prayers of the faithful? We can't know that for certain either. But we know, in this case, God used prayer to show his goodness and to build the faith and produce thanksgiving in the hearts of his followers. As believers, we can have faith that God does answer the prayers of those who truly believe and rely on him.

it's in the Bible

Throughout history, God's people have faced hard times. Elisha was a prophet of God, and believers often turned to him for advice.

During a time when kings battled each other in war, ordinary people struggled too. One day, a widow (a woman who had lost her husband to death) came to Elisha. If she did not get money, her two sons would be taken as slaves. Elisha asked this mother to take a step of faith, and this is what happened:

> The wife of a man from the company of the prophets cried out to Elisha, "Your servant my husband is dead, and you know that he revered the LORD. But now his creditor is coming to take my two boys as his slaves."
>
> Elisha replied to her, "How can I help you? Tell me, what do you have in your house?"
>
> "Your servant has nothing there at all," she said, "except a small jar of olive oil."
>
> Elisha said, "Go around and ask all your neighbors for empty jars. Don't ask for just a few. Then go inside and shut the door behind you and your sons. Pour oil into all the jars, and as each is filled, put it to one side."
>
> She left him and shut the door behind her and her

sons. They brought the jars to her and she kept pouring. When all the jars were full, she said to her son, "Bring me another one."

But he replied, "There is not a jar left." Then the oil stopped flowing.

She went and told the man of God, and he said, "Go, sell the oil and pay your debts. You and your sons can live on what is left." —2 Kings 4:1–7

Sometimes we think that miracles can't happen, but the truth is that we often forget to pray for them. Praying takes humility. Turning to God means that we don't have the answers ourselves. Yet when God answers in amazing ways, we have much to be thankful for.

Your Life

Do you pray and ask God for small things or big things? Often we only ask small prayers, ones we're sure that God can answer. But the truth is that God can answer big prayers just as easily as he can answer small ones. What matters is that you humble yourself before him, realizing that he is the one who knows best.

Also, when we pray, it's important to look at our own hearts. God doesn't answer selfish prayers, but when we pray with pure motives and a pure heart, it's amazing what can happen.

God can answer prayers in astonishing ways.

CHAPTER 8

JOHN ELIOT

Reaching People Where They Are

Private Collection/Peter Newark American Pictures/Bridgeman Images

When He Lived: 1604 – 1690 AD

⟶ **1646 AD**

John Eliot preaches the first sermon to the Native Americans in Algonquin

John Eliot scanned the crowd. A sea of Indian faces looked at him. He'd been in America for fifteen years, and he'd accomplished many things. Nothing, though, was as

75

great as the task set before him. These people knew very little about Jesus Christ or God's Word. John had worked hard to learn their language, and now was his chance to tell them the truth that would change everything.

John opened his mouth to speak. He was using the native language, and as he looked around he could tell that the people understood him. Ever since he'd first arrived in New England, John had prayed for the native people. He prayed that they would know God's truth and share it with others. As John shared passages from God's Word, he hoped they would take root and spread.

The truth of God's Word was something John had known from his earliest days. The Bible teaches parents to "train up a child in the way he should go," and that was the case with John Eliot. He couldn't remember a minute of his life when he did not know about God's love, and he could thank his parents for that.

John's first years were filled with fearing God, learning the Bible, and prayer. John grew up and graduated from the University of Cambridge. He was an excellent Bible student and he could have gone anywhere, but he chose to travel to America. He arrived in Boston in 1631.

In America, God used John greatly. John and two friends translated the book of Psalms into English, and the Bay Psalm Book became the first book printed in America.[35]

While the needs of the first settlers were great, John's attention turned to the native people. God's Words were in his thoughts: "Go out into all the world to preach."

John's first task was to learn the language of the twenty tribes who lived in and around the colonies. John learned the language, and now the real work was ready to begin.

On October 28, 1646, before his first sermon, John knelt in prayer. "Dear Lord, please make today's preaching successful."

It was no ordinary congregation that John was preaching to. It was the first American Indian audience to hear the Gospel of Christ.

But the preaching was just the beginning of John's vision. In his mind's eye, John pictured them understanding God's grace and love through the Scriptures. He could preach to limited crowds, but the Holy Bible would go out where he could not. John also knew that for their faith to continue, they had to teach each other. Parents must raise children to know and love God, just as his parents did with him.

In 1649, John proposed to translate parts of the Bible into the native language. The King James Version of the Bible had been published thirty-eight years before. Why shouldn't the Native Americans have God's Word in their language too?

John's passion for God amazed the native peoples. Many of them became followers of Jesus, and those all over New England heard of John's great work.

As a missionary, John tried to gather Native Americans into planned towns. At one point, there were fourteen towns of so-called "Praying Indians."

In 1660, the first Native American church was organized in Natick, Massachusetts, but not everyone was happy. The Indian sachem (leader) Cutshamokin didn't trust the new religion at first. However, John Eliot told the sachem he was there to do God's work. Cutshamokin respected Eliot's persistence and calmly discussed his concerns. Soon the two of them resolved the issue, and the next praying town was established.

In 1661, John Eliot translated the New Testament into the native language, and by 1664, he'd translated the whole Bible into Algonquin. One thousand copies were printed.[36]

The translation was not easy. The longest word in the Indian Bible was *wutappesittukqussunnoohwehtunkquoh*. It meant, "kneeling down to him," and was found in Mark 1:40.[37]

What John accomplished was a miracle. The King James Version of the Bible took fifty-four men seven years to create, but John completed his translation in only fourteen years, working only with some Algonquin interpreters who advised him on their lexicography.

He went on to work on Indian grammar books and catechism. One of the last things he wrote was *Brief Narrative of the Progress of the Gospel amongst the Indians in New England, in the Year 1670*. By 1675, 2,500 native people had become Christians.

John died on May 21, 1690. His last words were, "Welcome, joy." But John's passion for the native people of New England lived on.

In a June 14, 1906 edition of the New York Observer, the testimony of John's life was shared to encourage others to become missionaries: "There is much that can be done for our Indians west of the Mississippi. Men of the Eliot type and spirit are needed in Arizona, New Mexico, Idaho, and Montana ... Hundreds of men filled with the Christ spirit are laboring earnestly among the Indians today. Let us do our part to encourage missionary endeavor."[38]

John Eliot became the first missionary to the Native

Americans, and his example encouraged many to follow in his footsteps. Because of him, thousands of Native Americans learned about the one true God, and history was forever changed.

The ends of the earth shall turn to him

John's greatest joy was seeing the Indian people come to know Jesus Christ. In a letter to a friend, John talked about visiting with a sachem and returning back to one of the wigwams. As he approached, John heard a native in prayer. "Though I could not understand but little of his words, and consider that God was fulfilling his Word, vis. The ends of the earth shall remember themselves and turne unto him; and that Scripture, 'Thou art the God that hearest prayer, unto thee shall all flesh come.'" (Quoting from Psalm 65:2).[39]

Another Bible verse that speaks about this is Psalm 86:9, "All the nations you have made will come and worship before you, Lord; they will bring glory to your name" (NIV).

Because of people with missionary hearts like John Eliot, men, women, and children around the world now have come to worship before our great King, Jesus Christ.

Something to Think About

God desires people from all over the world to hear the Good News of Jesus. When did you first hear? John's parents were the first ones to tell him about Jesus. Who was the first person to share with you? How can you pray that more people around the world can hear about Jesus? What can you do?

In His Own Words

John Eliot's book about his time as a missionary is now considered an important historical document. Here are John's words about the changes that happened when the native people of New England heard the good news of Jesus Christ.

Upon the 17th day of the 6th month, 1670, there was a Meeting at Maktapog near Sandwich in Plimouth-Pattent, to gather a Church among the Indians: There were present six of the Magistrates, and many Elders, (all of them Messengers of the Churches within that Jurisdiction) in whose presence, in a day of Fasting and Prayer, they making confession of the Truth and Grace of Jesus Christ, did in that solemn Assembly enter into Covenant, to walk together in the Faith and Order of the Gospel; and were accepted and declared to be a Church of Jesus Christ. These Indians being of kin to our Massachuset-Indians who first prayed unto God, conversed with them, and received amongst them the light and love of the Truth.[40]

It's amazing how many changes can happen among a people when one man chooses to follow God, to pray, and to go to the people God has called him to.

How He Changed History

John Eliot's contribution to history wasn't solely that he brought Christianity to the Native Americans, but that he also brought them literacy. One of the reasons Europeans saw the natives as "uncivilized" was because they did not have a form of writing. Eliot's use of the native language in his translation efforts allowed them to develop one. John Eliot also gave them the most wonderful book to read when he translated the Bible into their own language.

It's in the Bible

The early apostles give us an example of what it's like to travel to foreign places to share the gospel.

In the book of Acts, Paul travels a long distance to share the news of Jesus. When he gets to Athens, Paul looks around and uses items that the people who live there can understand. He uses an idol to the "Unknown God" as a tool to preach to the people about the God who made the heavens and the earth.

> So Paul, standing before the council, addressed them as follows: "Men of Athens, I notice that you are very religious in every way, for as I was walking along I saw your many shrines. And one of your altars had this inscription on it: 'To an Unknown God.' This God, whom you worship without knowing, is the one I'm telling you about."
>
> —Acts 17:22–23 (NLT)

Paul went on to tell the people who this unknown God was.

> He is the God who made the world and everything
> in it. Since he is Lord of heaven and earth, he doesn't
> live in man-made temples, and human hands can't serve
> his needs—for he has no needs. He himself gives life and
> breath to everything, and he satisfies every need. From
> one man he created all the nations throughout the whole
> earth. He decided beforehand when they should rise and
> fall, and he determined their boundaries.
>
> —Acts 17:24–26 (NLT)

Paul told the people that the one true God was not made by craftsmen. He was not made of wood or stone. Instead God commands everyone to repent of their sins and turn to him. The people listened, and some became believers. But others laughed when they heard that Jesus rose from the dead.

Paul used this idol to an "Unknown God" as a way to tell his listeners about Jesus. John Eliot learned the language of the Algonquin in order to share the same message. Not all who heard Paul believed. Not all who heard John Eliot believed either. Yet some did, and that's what matters most. Whether 1 or 100 believe in Jesus isn't important. Instead, doing what God asked and following him is.

Today, people all over the world still need to hear about Jesus. Sometimes God calls us to go where they are, and when we do, God will show us how to share his love in a way the people will understand. When we do our job, God will do his.

Your Life

Have you ever considered that God can use you to tell others about him? God can use you in amazing ways when you choose to follow him. Consider praying and asking God who he wants you to share his good news with. It might be someone next door. Or maybe, when you're older, it might be someone in a different country. Your job isn't to make people change. Your job is simply to share about Jesus and let them know that change—with God's help— is possible.

People need to hear the good news of Jesus, no matter where they live or what they believe.

CHAPTER 9

SUSANNA WESLEY

Prayers for Her Children

Classic Image/Alamy

When She Lived: 1669 – 1742 AD

→ 1708 AD

Susanna Wesley commits to pray, and her children grow strong in the Lord

Susanna Wesley took in a deep breath and blew it out slowly. Her house was filled with noise ... and with children. Susanna had given birth to nineteen children, though only ten lived to be adults. Two of her sons, John and Charles Wesley, grew up to be two of the greatest pastors who ever lived. Their messages brought millions of souls to Christ. But as Susanna was caring for many children— with very little money—she could not have known that. All she knew was that she needed help, so she turned to God in prayer.

Susanna's husband, Samuel Wesley, spent time in jail twice due to his poor financial choices, and their lack of money was a continual struggle for Susanna. Her family's life was filled with obstacles. Their house burned down twice. During one of the fires, her son John nearly died and had to be rescued from a second-story window. She was the primary source of her children's education.[41]

When Susanna was young, she had promised the Lord that for every hour spent in entertainment she would give him the same amount of time in prayer and in the Word. This was hard to do with so many children and responsibilities. As a woman during that time period, she had to do all the chores by hand, teach the children, and manage the entire household. In addition to that, her family was always in debt. Because they couldn't afford much, Susanna started raising animals for food.

The milk, meat, and eggs that came from their little farmstead helped out financially, but they still weren't enough. As Susanna grew busier, she had been drifting away from God. She prayed each day and had taught the children the Lord's Prayer as soon as they could speak. But she didn't feel close to God. She wasn't making time for him, and Susanna felt empty inside.

Susanna thought about her pledge as a child. She had very little time for entertainment, and that meant very little time for prayer. So Susanna made a new pledge. Even with five small children, and teaching Sammy and Emilia six hours a day, she promised God two hours a day in prayer.[42]

It was hard for Susanna to get away to pray, so she told her children that if they saw her with her apron over her head that she was praying and should not be disturbed.

She prayed about many things, but mostly for her children. John and Charles ended up impacting a generation. John Wesley preached to nearly a million people. At the age of seventy he preached to 32,000 followers, without the use of a microphone. Charles Wesley wrote over 9,000 hymns, many of which we still sing today.

Susanna Wesley's situation in life caused her to pray often and fervently. Her children saw her praying, and it changed them. Susanna's prayers led to great things, namely her sons' passion to share the good news of Jesus Christ with others, and history was forever changed.

When we don't have time to pray, we need to make more time for it

Susanna Wesley had many struggles in her life, which meant she needed to pray a lot. Thankfully God is there when we turn to him. Here are a few verses that remind us of that:

"Look to the LORD and his strength; seek his face always" (1 Chronicles 16:11).

"The LORD is near to all who call on him, to all who call on him in truth" (Psalm 145:18).

As Susanna Wesley prayed, God answered her in many ways. Sometimes he provided in outward ways, and sometimes he strengthened Susanna on the inside. Either way, her children had front row seats to seeing God at work. And Susanna's children grew up to do great things with God's strength.

Something to Think About

Who is an example of someone devoted to prayer in your life? What have you learned about prayer from this book so far? How much time can you set aside to pray each day? How do you think taking time to pray will change you?

In Her Own Words

John Wesley once said, "I learned more about Christianity from my mother than from all the theologians in England." He asked his mother to write a little on the way she raised the children. This is what she had to say:

> The children of this family were taught, as soon as they could speak, the Lord's Prayer, which they were made to say at rising and bed-time constantly; to which, as they grew bigger, were added a short prayer for their parents, and some collects; a short catechism, and some portion of Scripture, as their memories could bear.
>
> They were very early made to distinguish the Sabbath from other days; before they could well speak or go. They were as soon taught to be still at family prayers, and to ask a blessing immediately after, which they used to do by signs, before they could kneel or speak.[43]

The Wesley children learned to take prayer seriously because their mother taught them to.

How She Changed History

Susanna provided an example of spiritual dedication and unwavering faith to her children. As a result of her godly example, her two sons became pastors, and Charles and John are credited with founding the Methodist movement. The orderly system of Methodism was influenced by Susanna's well-organized style of child rearing, in which discipline, respect, and prayer were the backbones. Susanna's dedicated prayers for her children helped expand the Christian faith in ways she couldn't have imagined.

it's in the Bible

No one is born knowing how to pray. Prayer is something we must learn. Even Jesus' disciples asked him to teach them how to pray. And this is what Jesus told them in Luke 11:1–13 (NLT):

> *Once Jesus was in a certain place praying. As he finished, one of his disciples came to him and said, "Lord, teach us to pray, just as John taught his disciples."*
> *Jesus said, "This is how you should pray:*
> *"Father, may your name be kept holy.*
> *May your Kingdom come soon.*
> *Give us each day the food we need,*
> *and forgive us our sins,*
> *as we forgive those who sin against us.*
> *And don't let us yield to temptation."*
> *Then, teaching them more about prayer, he used this story: "Suppose you went to a friend's house at midnight,*

wanting to borrow three loaves of bread. You say to him, 'A friend of mine has just arrived for a visit, and I have nothing for him to eat. And suppose he calls out from his bedroom, 'Don't bother me. The door is locked for the night, and my family and I are all in bed. I can't help you.' But I tell you this—though he won't do it for friendship's sake, if you keep knocking long enough, he will get up and give you whatever you need because of your shameless persistence.

"And so I tell you, keep on asking, and you will receive what you ask for. Keep on seeking, and you will find. Keep on knocking, and the door will be opened to you. For everyone who asks, receives. Everyone who seeks, finds. And to everyone who knocks, the door will be opened.

"You fathers—if your children ask for a fish, do you give them a snake instead? Or if they ask for an egg, do you give them a scorpion? Of course not! So if you sinful people know how to give good gifts to your children, how much more will your heavenly Father give the Holy Spirit to those who ask him."

Whenever we wonder how to pray, we can turn back to Jesus' words. Whenever we wonder if prayer matters, we can turn back to Jesus' words … again.

Your Life

Do you need someone to teach you how to pray? Take time thinking about who that could be. Who is a wonderful example of prayer and devotion in your life? A parent? A grandparent? A Sunday school teacher? Approach that person and ask if he or she can teach you to pray too.

When we pray, our prayers change things ... and sometimes they change the people watching us most.

CHAPTER 10

JOHN NEWTON

God Transforms Lives

Private Collection/Bridgeman Images

When He Lived: 1725 – 1807 AD

→ **1748 AD**

John comes close to death in a storm and discovers God's mercy

Fear coursed through John Newton's body. He'd faced many a storm — some worse than others — but never one like this.

The son of a sea captain, John went to sea himself at eleven years old. He'd traveled the Mediterranean and to the West Indies as a sailor.

John had gone to bed the night before on his ship the *Greyhound* without a care in the world, but he awoke with the thrashing of the sea. Sheets of rain poured down. The crew was facing a severe storm off the coast of Donegal, Ireland. High water pounded the ship. Torrential waves swept over the deck, and soon John's cabin was filled with water.

As John struggled through the icy streams, a cry came from on deck, "The ship's going down!" The strong winds that had pushed the Greyhound westward now slammed against the ship.

Before this day, the ship had been in African waters for fifteen months. Her timbers were rotted and her sails were worn.[44]

John struggled up onto the deck, and a captain met him at the ropes.

"John, can you get a knife?" the captain called.

John left to retrieve a knife, and at the same time another person took John's place. Upon reaching the deck, a violent wave washed that same man overboard. John didn't have time to think about the man—or that it should have been him. The ship was filling up with water, and he had to act fast.

Up on deck, John saw that the sea had torn away the upper timbers on one side. The beautiful ship was nothing more than a wreck.

The crew manned the pumps, but more water rushed in than could be bailed out. John moved to another part of the vessel and set to work with buckets and pails. A dozen people worked with all their might. Water filled near to the ceiling, and John was astonished the ship didn't sink. Then he remembered their cargo was made up of bees' wax and light African camwood—much lighter than water.

Within a few hours, morning light stretched its arms across the water. Soon the winds stilled, and the men used their clothes and bedding to stop the leaks. They worked as quickly as they could, nailing boards over the holes.

Weariness caused John's bones to ache. His energy was

nearly gone. With the last of his strength, he sought out the captain to update him on the condition of the ship.

"If this will not do, the Lord have mercy upon us." John said.[45]

The words were said without much thought at first, but they continued to play through John's mind. *Mercy! Mercy!*

What mercy can there be for me?

It was the first time he'd thought of God's mercy for many years. He didn't understand it. Instead of the curses that he usually spoke, he had spoken God's name in reverence.

His close call with death caused him to think of God even as he worked on the pump, trying to get more of the water out of the ship. He pumped for hours, and waves continued to wash over him. The sailors tied themselves fast with ropes, but John still wondered if it was enough. Nearly every time the ship lowered into the sea, John worried it would never rise again.

John had always dreaded death, but now his heart was heavy with fear. He'd turned his back on God's Word, but now—with the sea raging around him—John questioned if he should reconsider.

Around 6:00 p.m., when the extra water had been removed from the ship, hope arose in John's heart. It was then that he began to pray.

I could not utter the prayer of faith; I could not draw near to a reconciled God, and call him Father; my prayer was like the cry of the ravens, which yet the Lord does not disdain to hear. I now began to think of that Jesus whom I had so often derided; I recollected the particulars of his life, and of his death; a death for sins not his own – but, as I remembered, for the sake of those who, in their distress, would put their trust in him. And how I chiefly wanted evidence.[46]

What if the Christian faith was true? John's new prayer was that he would come to know.

Over the next six years, John discovered the evil in his heart. He continued to work on slave ships, transporting men and women, but often wondered, *Should I be doing this?*

John read the Bible many times, and he tried to understand God's truth. But true change came after John struck up a friendship with a captain who was a member of a highly respected church. For the next month, they spent nearly every evening together, meeting on each other's ships. They met and talked about the Bible, and sometimes they talked through the night until morning. Many of John's questions were answered.

Through his friend, John learned about grace and learned more about what faith in the Lord was all about. Yet at this time, John Newton was still involved in the slave trade. His cargo was men and women in chains, bolts, and shackles. The more John got to know God's Word—and God's love—the more he started praying that God would give him a job that didn't hurt people.

From that point on, he stopped cursing, gambling, and drinking. John no longer liked his work, and he didn't like being far from home for so long.

John's prayer was answered, but not in the way he expected. Just a few days before setting sail, he was having tea with his wife when he had a seizure that left him unable to move. He recovered after an hour but continued to have symptoms. John's doctor suggested he shouldn't sail, and John walked away from his position as a captain the day before he was to leave on his next voyage.

John soon discovered that God's hand was upon him. Another storm hit the ship he was supposed to be on. The person who took his place, most of the officers, and many of the crew died.

John continued to be ill, and when he got better, his wife came down with an unknown illness and grew worse day by day. No doctor could discover what was wrong. Yet after John committed all that he was to the Lord, his wife grew better.

John finally turned his life over fully to God. He not only walked away from the wrong he had done, but he started living for God in amazing ways. The former slave ship captain also fought against slavery.

One of John's favorite verses was Galatians 1:23, "That he which persecuted us in times past now preacheth the faith which once he destroyed" (KJV).

John had once transported slaves, but his new role became to preach and tell people about the freedom from their sins that can be found in Jesus Christ.

In 1764, John began to preach and write hymns. This once vile sailor even ended up writing one of the most famous hymns of all, "Amazing Grace." Because of a prayer at sea that started a transformation in John Newton's life, the slave trade, music, and history were forever changed.

We're not what we used to be

John Newton is quoted as saying, "I am not what I ought to be, I am not what I want to be, I am not what I hope to be in another world; but still I am not what I once used to be, and by the grace of God I am what I am."

God's Word talks about this too: "Whoever is a believer in Christ is a new creation. The old way of living has disappeared. A new way of living has come into existence" (2 Corinthians 5:17 God's Word).

Aren't we thankful that we don't have to carry all our heavy sins around? Aren't we thankful that we can give them to Jesus?

Something to Think About

What does it mean to be a new creation? How do you know if you're different on the inside? And if you're different on the inside, what changes happen on the outside too?

In His Own Words

Before he died, John Newton prepared his own epitaph (a summary of his life). Here is a portion of it:

John Newton, once an infidel and libertine, a servant of slaves in Africa was, by the rich mercy of our Lord and Saviour, Jesus Christ, preserved, restored, pardoned, and appointed to preach the faith he had long laboured to destroy...[47]

John also wrote one of the most popular hymns of all time. Can you see his thankfulness for God's mercy in these lines?

> Amazing grace! (how sweet the sound!)
> That saved a wretch like me;
> I once was lost, but now am found;
> Was blind, but now I see.

How He Changed History

John Newton was not a "perfect" Christian. Even after becoming a Christian, he made money off of the slave trade. Later in his life, he realized that he could not be a true Christian and support slavery. His greatest impact on world changes was his influence on William Wilberforce, who would become the leader of the movement to end slavery in Britain. In his pamphlet "Thoughts Upon the Slave Trade," Newton tells of the awful conditions on slave ships that he saw firsthand. This work inspired Wilberforce, a member of parliament, to fight to outlaw the slave trade in Great Britain.

The more John Newton understood about God's love, grace, and freedom in his own life, the more he was able to open his heart and help others understand love, grace, and freedom for the lives of slaves too.

it's in the Bible

Often great men in Christian history have dark pasts that they are ashamed of. Just like John Newton, Saul (later Paul) struck out against humanity. John carried Africans in slave ships. Saul's mission was to destroy the early Christian church.

A devout Jew, Saul got permission from the chief priests to arrest all the followers of Jesus—those who belonged to "the Way." He went from house to house, arresting men and women. He had them put in prison. One day on the road to Damascus, Jesus spoke to Saul and changed his heart.

> When he got to the outskirts of Damascus, he was suddenly dazed by a blinding flash of light. As he fell to the ground, he heard a voice: "Saul, Saul, why are you out to get me?"
>
> He said, "Who are you, Master?"
>
> "I am Jesus, the One you're hunting down. I want you to get up and enter the city. In the city you'll be told what to do next."
>
> His companions stood there dumbstruck—they could hear the sound, but couldn't see anyone—while Saul, picking himself up off the ground, found himself stone-blind. They had to take him by the hand and lead him into Damascus. He continued blind for three days. He ate nothing, drank nothing.   —Acts 9:3–9 (MSG)

Just as God was making himself known to Saul, he sent a vision to a disciple in Damascus named Ananias, too. In the vision, God told Ananias to go to a house on Straight Avenue, where Saul was. This didn't make Ananias happy.

Ananias protested, "Master, you can't be serious. Everybody's talking about this man and the terrible things he's been doing, his reign of terror against your people in Jerusalem! And now he's shown up here with papers from the Chief Priest that give him license to do the same to us."

But the Master said, "Don't argue. Go! I have picked him as my personal representative to non-Jews and kings and Jews. And now I'm about to show him what he's in for—the hard suffering that goes with this job."

So Ananias went and found the house, placed his hands on blind Saul, and said, "Brother Saul, the Master sent me, the same Jesus you saw on your way here. He sent me so you could see again and be filled with the Holy Spirit." No sooner were the words out of his mouth than something like scales fell from Saul's eyes—he could see again! He got to his feet, was baptized, and sat down with them to a hearty meal."   —Acts 9:13–18 (MSG)

Saul became Paul—a great missionary who traveled the world sharing the good news of Jesus. How amazing is that?

Sometimes those who've had the biggest changes in their hearts work hardest to share the Good News of Jesus. After all, if God can make such beautiful changes within them, then he can do the same for others. Yet for this to happen, we must humble ourselves in prayer and depend on God's mercy.

Your Life

Each one of us has sinned against God. Some sins seem bigger and some seem smaller, yet to God they are all the same. Instead of trying to do things our own way, we need to realize our need for God's mercy. Then, once we accept God's mercy in our lives, we can share it with others.

Sometimes God uses unlikely people to share news of his mercy and forgiveness.

CHAPTER 11

ROBERT RAIKES

Good News for Children

When He Lived: 1736 – 1811 AD

→ **1780 AD**

Robert Raikes starts the first Sunday school to help street children

Robert Raikes walked down the street in Gloucester, England, heading to Sunday services. Like most men of his day, he wore a full-bottomed powdered wig, and over it, a black three-cornered hat. His coat had large pockets and a long waist that hung far below his knees. It was the Sabbath, but no one would know it by the commotion. The streets were filled with a noisy racket.

The children in these parts worked in the pin factory during the week. On Sundays, the factory people and the working men had the day off, but instead of going to church or resting at home, many people did not make good use of their time.[48]

Trouble was brewing at every corner. The children were

disrespectful, fought each other, and swore terribly. The children didn't have much education. They also didn't have many people who cared for them or wanted to help them grow up right. If they continued on this path of making wrong choices, where would they end up?

Robert had worked in the prisons trying to help criminals. He knew that's exactly where the children would be when they got older if things didn't change.

But what could he do? Robert believed that if the children could receive the Lord's instruction, it would make all the difference in their lives. Unfortunately, the poorer children of the city never made it to the church pews. Neither did their parents. Their parents had struggles of their own, like trying to feed and clothe their families. Also, many of these children were orphans who did not have parents to serve as examples for them.

Robert thought hard about what he could do. What if someone stepped forward to reach out to them and invite them to church? What if someone were to make a point to instill good principles in their minds?[49]

Robert approached some of the parents of these children. They quickly agreed for the children to meet him at the cathedral on Sunday mornings. At first, very few children showed up, but then more and more came. Slowly but surely, they were drawn to Robert's kind and gentle nature. It was unlike what they knew from the streets. Soon, Robert had a parade of ragamuffins following him every Sunday morning. The kids' behavior and attitudes began to improve. Robert taught them to kneel, stand, and sit down in the different parts of service.[50]

But as soon as the church service was over, the children

were back on the streets, running wild. The more time he spent with the children, the more Robert realized that he could do more for them than just teach them how to behave during the Sunday service. He began to consider what he could do—with the help of others—to give the children a Christian education.

Robert met with friends and shared his vision. In a short amount of time, money was raised for children to be taught on Sunday afternoons. Robert next talked to four women. Each of them agreed to teach the children reading and Bible for a minimal wage. A day or two after talking to the teachers, he met the Reverend Thomas Stock.

"I wish something could be done for those unfortunate children in your parish, Mr. Stock; their behaviour and language on the Sabbath is, I am told, horribly profane and disgusting. Have you ever noticed it?"[51]

The Reverend agreed there was a great need. The two men prayed together. They prayed that God would open a way for these children to be educated in God's Word.

Then the gentlemen walked to the part of the city of Gloucester that was inhabited by thieves, housebreakers, and highway robbers. They approached the parents there, telling them of this new opportunity. The parents were eager to have their children attend.

Ninety children soon started attending classes taught by the four teachers. Their textbook was the Bible. The first Sunday meeting of these poor, neglected children took place at the house of Mr. King on St. Catherine Street, in July 1780.[52] Six months later, more schools were established all over the city. The children not only learned how to be respectful on the outside, but as they grew to know about Jesus, their hearts changed, too.

Soon, as Robert walked down the streets on Sunday afternoons, there was peace. The lying, swearing, and recklessness were replaced by honesty and truth. It didn't take much to direct the children. The smallest rewards went far. Even more effective was the smallest sign of displeasure from Robert. The children wanted to please him, and they worked hard to be better for him.

In 1777, Robert was appointed headmaster of the Gloucester Cathedral School. Within four years, 250,000 students were attending the Bible classes. By Robert's death in 1811, 500,000 attended. By 1831, 1.25 million children attended "Sunday School" in cities throughout Great Britain. God's Word changed them inside and out, and history was forever changed.

Starting small can grow to greater things

When Robert Raikes started his Sunday schools, he had only four Sunday school teachers. Now there are hundreds of thousands—maybe millions—of Sunday school teachers around the world.

Zechariah 4:10 says, "Do not despise these small beginnings, for the LORD rejoices to see the work begin" (NLT).

When God places a need in front of you, it is a time to act. Robert Raikes is an example of that. When you act, even in small ways, you never know how God is going to use your actions. Because Robert was willing to start small, God was able to use him to do great things.

Something to Think About

What are the things you are most concerned about? What small thing is God asking you to do? What is one way that you can pray for God to do a small thing through you?

In His Own Words

Robert's heart wasn't captured by the street children alone. His prayers also went up for those in prison. He reached out to those who were incarcerated in the county Poor Law (part of the jail at that time).[53] He wrote this about a young man who was executed at the jail for breaking into someone's house: "He had never received the smallest instruction. He had never offered up a prayer to his Creator. He said he knew not how to pray. He was totally devoid of all sense of a future state."[54]

Robert saw the Sunday schools as a way to prevent children from ending up living a life in prison. Robert knew that teaching children to know God and how to pray would make all the difference. And it did.

How He Changed History

By 1831, Sunday schools taught about 25 percent of the British children. These Sunday schools laid the groundwork for the public school system in England. Because of the godly education that the children received, crime lessened on the streets. The children's behavior began to improve.

Robert understood that to change history he had to change children. He said, "The world marches forth on the feet of little children."[55] As God's glory is promoted to children, seeds of faith, truth, and goodness are sown in their hearts. These values grow as the children do, changing the next generation and the society around them.

It's in the Bible

In Biblical days, people didn't pay much attention to children. But when Jesus was on earth, parents everywhere wanted to bring their little ones to see him.

When the disciples saw the parents coming with their children, they told the parents to leave Jesus alone. Jesus wasn't happy about that at all.

> *One day some parents brought their little children to Jesus so he could touch and bless them. But the disciples scolded the parents for bothering him.*
>
> *When Jesus saw what was happening, he was angry with his disciples. He said to them, "Let the children come to me. Don't stop them! For the Kingdom of God belongs to those who are like these children. I tell you the truth, anyone who doesn't receive the Kingdom of God like a child will never enter it."*
>
> —*Mark 10:13–15 (NLT)*

Jesus gathered the little children around him with joy. This showed something very important: The old way of doing things was over. The good news was for children too. Jesus also told his disciples they needed to be more like the children in their faith.

The children were allowed to be with Jesus, and they became an example for the adults too. When faith is planted in a child's heart, it grows. Soon "little" becomes "much" because of Jesus.

Your Life

Sometimes it seems as if kids go unnoticed. The wonderful thing is that God notices children. Even more, he welcomes them to come to him. Whenever you feel as if you aren't understood, God understands. He's there for you.

God cares about children going through hard times. Even though there are people who seem rough on the outside, they need to hear about Jesus too. Just like Robert Raikes, if you know someone like this, consider inviting that person to church. And also like Robert Raikes, start by praying for them first. You never know how that person can change as they learn about God and what a relationship with him means.

God invites even children to hear his Good News.

CHAPTER 12

MARY JONES

God Uses Unlikely People

When She Lived: 1784 – 1864 AD

→ 1800 AD

Mary gives all she has to get one Bible, and God uses her passion to take Bibles to millions

Mary Jones straightened her shoulders and pretended to act older than her fifteen years. She smiled and waved to a man with a peasant cart who was walking in the opposite direction.

"Dear Lord, give me strength." She wiped her brow as the sun beat down on her forehead.

She was nearing the end of her twenty-five miles. Her heartbeat quickened as she thought that soon she'd finally have a Welsh Bible of her own.

Ever since Mary had become a follower of Jesus Christ at age eight, she'd looked forward to this day. She'd learned to read, and she knew of a Bible at a farm two miles away. Many times a week, Mary walked the two miles just to read the Bible for herself. It was worth the travel, but more than anything she wanted a Bible of her own.

Bibles in the Welsh language were rare. There wasn't a Bible for sale anywhere near Mary, but now she hoped to find one in the town of Bala. Did she dare hope that God would grant her favor and she'd be able to find one?

It had taken her six years to save enough money. This journey was the last thing to conquer before she'd achieve her goal. Her bare feet were filthy from the trip, but a glimmer of hope rose in her heart. Soon, she might have a copy of her own.

Her father was a poor weaver, and he had died when she was only four. Many of the household duties had become Mary's responsibility as her mother worked.[56] They lived in a small cottage at the foot of the Cader Idris Mountain.

Now their cottage was far behind, and Mary thanked God that the journey to Bala had been uneventful so far. She still worried, would a Bible be available after she'd gone all this way?

Mary had asked everyone she knew about where she could buy a Bible of her own. There was no one near Bala who had a Bible, but she was told that some Welsh Bibles had been printed in Oxford last year that had been given to a man named Mr. Charles at a very reasonable price by the Religious Tract Society in London. She feared that they had all been sold or promised months ago.[57]

She prayed again that Mr. Charles would have a Bible to sell.

It took all day for Mary to travel to Bala. Many people helped her along the way, sharing bits of food and water with her.

Upon arriving in town, Mary followed the directions she'd been given and went to the house of a Methodist preacher, Reverend David Edwards. She asked Reverend Edwards for directions to Mr. Charles' house. Since it was late, Reverend Edwards urged her to stay the night in his attic room and approach Mr. Charles the next day.

Reverend Edwards took her to the home of Mr. Charles. Her knees trembled as she finally stood before him.

"What do you need, dear child?" Mr. Charles asked.

Her words rushed out then. She told him about her mother and her home. She told him about believing in Jesus and wanting a Bible of her own. She even told him how she visited her friends at the farmhouse to read their Bible—and how she'd memorized as much as she could.

"I've saved up my money for many years. I have the money for my own Bible now, and I've come a long way ..."

"I'm sorry, Miss, I do not have any Bibles to sell. The Welsh Bibles that I received sold out quickly. I only have a few copies that I'm saving for friends."[58]

Mary's lower lip trembled. Tears flooded her eyes. "But I've waited so long. I've saved my money ..."

Her shoulders sank. She'd come so far.

Lord, what shall I do now?

Reverend Charles peered down at the young woman before him, and compassion filled his heart. He could tell from her garments that she had little money. He had also walked the path she'd taken the day before. The journey wasn't any easy one. This young woman had crossed valleys, forged rivers, and circled around mountains. And how long had she said she'd saved money? Six years! Her eyes, full of tears peered up at him, causing his own vision to blur. The Word of God was so precious to him, and the longing in this young girl's eyes was clear.

"My sweet child. I see that you must have a Bible," he finally said. "I will give you the Bible that I have promised another. I will find a way to order another Bible for my friend. Surely when I tell him of your patient endurance he will understand. I simply cannot refuse you."

Young Mary Jones wiped her tears. Dirt from her journey streaked her face, but her smile radiated joy.

Mr. Charles turned to the bookcase behind him and picked up a Bible, then handed it to Mary. She pressed it to her chest and more tears came, but these were happy tears.

After breakfast with Mr. Edwards, Mary Jones set off for the twenty-five miles home. There was a lightness to her step and a bright smile on her face.

That night, Thomas Charles tried to sleep, but he couldn't. He'd given much of his life to traveling around and teaching young people from poor families to read, but what good did it do if they didn't have the greatest literature of all, the Holy Bible. What could be done to help other people like Mary? How many people around the world longed for a Bible?

In the winter of 1802, Thomas Charles visited London. He gathered some of his closest friends and told them the idea burning in his heart. What if they set up a society to distribute God's Holy Word?

When talking to some of his friends from the Committee of the Religious Tract Society, he shared the story of the young girl Mary Jones. The men were moved, but they questioned if they should only provide Bibles for Wales.

"Mr. Charles, why stop at Wales?" one of his friends asked. "Why not for the whole world?"

In 1804, the British and Foreign Bible Society was established in London. It was with much joy and gratefulness that Mr. Charles learned that the first work of the Committee of the Bible Society would be to bring out an edition of the Welsh New Testament for Welsh Sunday schools.[59] Many people donated to provide Bibles, and most of the money came from poor peasants like Mary. The first New Testaments reached Bala in 1806, and a Welsh edition of the whole Bible arrived a year later.

A popular saying among the Welsh Christians was "A Bible for all the people in the world."

The work inspired by Mary grew, and by 1907, the Society had distributed hundreds of millions of Bibles all over the world. Because of the prayer of Mary Jones, a peasant girl, history was forever changed.[60]

God provides for our needs

The morning that she rose to go meet Mr. Charles, Mary thought of the 23rd Psalm, "The LORD is my shepherd; I have everything I need," Psalm 23:1 (NCV).

This verse was a reminder to Mary that she was cared for by a loving Shepherd. She knew God would be with her and lead her. What she didn't expect was how he would use her passion for his Word to bless so many other people. God not only had plans to get his Word into Mary's hands and heart, but also into the hands of those around the world.

Something to Think About

Do you ever think of God as your shepherd? In what ways has God provided what you need? Do you have your own Bible? What does owning a Bible mean to you?

In Her Own Words

Mary later married a weaver. She lived a simple life, yet she is still remembered. Today, her Bible is kept at the British and Foreign Bible Society's Archives in the Cambridge University Library. Within it are these words, written by Mary:

> Mary Jones was born 16th of December 1784.
> I Bought this in the 16th year of my age. I am Daughter of Jacob Jones and Mary Jones His wife. The Lord may give me grace. Amen.
> Mary Jones His [is] The True Onour [owner] of this Bible. Bought In the Year 1800 Aged 16th[61]

How She Changed History

Mary's thirst for knowledge and desire to read God's Word for herself inspired the creation of the British and Foreign Bible Society. The Society worked, and still works today, to make the Bible available to people in their own languages. During World War II, the Society delivered millions of copies of the Bible to soldiers in more than 80 languages. Their tireless work has contributed to the spread of Christianity and to literacy around the world.

It's in the Bible

A young boy named Josiah was only 8 years old when he became king of Israel. Years later, when the Word of God was brought to Josiah's attention, he read it and was changed by the message. Josiah then had the Bible read before all the people of Israel, and what happened after that was amazing:

> *Josiah was eight years old when he became king. He ruled for thirty-one years in Jerusalem. His mother's name was Jedidah daughter of Adaiah; she was from Bozkath. He lived the way GOD wanted. He kept straight on the path blazed by his ancestor David, not one step to either left or right.*   —2 Kings 22:1–2 (MSG)

Josiah walked in God's Ways because as a young boy he came to know God's words. He listened, paid attention, and then shared what he learned.

> *When the king heard what was written in the book, God's Revelation, he ripped his robes in dismay. And then he called for Hilkiah the priest, Ahikam son of Shaphan, Acbor son of Micaiah, Shaphan the royal secretary, and Asaiah the king's personal aide. He ordered them all: "Go and pray to GOD for me and for this people—for all Judah! Find out what we must do in response to what is written in this book that has just been found! GOD's anger must be burning furiously against us—our ancestors haven't obeyed a thing written in this book, followed none of the instructions directed to us.*   —2 Kings 22:11–13 (MSG)

Upon reading the laws of the Lord, Josiah asked for prayers for himself and for all of Judah. He not only read the Word of God for himself, but he also gathered all the people to listen to God's Word.

Because Josiah was eager for the people to know—and live by—God's Word, his country was changed. This shows that young people can make a difference.

When Mary Jones' heart burned with the desire for a Bible of her own, she prayed. She also saved her money and traveled long distances to obtain her precious Bible. Because of her determination, Mary received the Word of God, and millions of others did too, through the work of the Bible Society.

When young people, like Josiah and Mary Jones, are passionate about the Word of God and go to the Lord in prayer, many, many lives can be transformed.

Your Life

Do you get excited about reading your Bible? The more you grow in God's Word, the more others will get excited about it too. God can use anyone to share his Good News. Even though you are young, you can make a difference too.

Sometimes God uses those who are young to spread the Good News.

CHAPTER 13

SOJOURNER TRUTH

We Can Pray for Our Families

When She Lived: 1797 – 1883 AD

→ 1826 AD

Sojourner Truth pleads with God for favor in getting her son out of slavery

Sojourner Truth had prayed more times than she could count over the years. She was born into slavery in Swartekill, Ulster County, New York.[62] Maybe her most fervent prayers happened when she was a small girl and part of a slave auction. At the time, her name was Isabella, and she was sold for one hundred dollars to John Nealy of Ulster County, New York.[63] She was scared when her master took her to her new home.

Isabella had a hard life with her new masters. During that first winter, her feet were badly frozen because of the cold. She had plenty to eat, but she also got plenty of whippings. Her masters were horribly cruel.

"Oh! My God!" she cried, "What a way is this of treating human beings?"[64]

Thankfully, Isabella had a chance to escape slavery. She was promised her freedom, and when the time came, she left. But just before that she also lost something precious to her.

Shortly before Isabella left her master, he sold her son Peter. Isabella's five-year-old boy was sold to a man named Dr. Gedney, who took Peter with him as far as New York City, on his way to England.

Finding the boy too small for his service, Dr. Gedney sent him back to his brother, Solomon Gedney. This man disposed of him to his sister's husband, a wealthy planter by the name of Fowler, who took him to his own home in Alabama.[65]

Isabella heard that her son had been sold and that he was now in the south. At the time, it was illegal to sell a child out of the state. So, she pleaded for help from her former mistress, who thought Isabella was making a lot of commotion for one child.

Isabella squared her shoulders. "I'll have my child again."

"Have your child again?" the mistress said. The idea seemed absurd to her. "How can you get him? And what have you to support him with, if you could? Have you any money?"

"No," said Isabella. "I have no money, but God has enough, or what's better. And I'll have my child again."

And as she walked away, Isabella was sure her words were true. She felt so tall within—as if the power of the nation was with her. The American Revolution had been fought for a reason, and she believed this small war would be won too.[66]

Yet as the days passed, a heavy darkness covered Isabella's heart. How would she ever find Peter again? She finally talked to a man who told her to go to the Quakers, who were already upset that her son had been sold in such a way. They took pity on Isabella and promised to help her. And that night, for the first time in her life, she slept in a nice, clean, white, and beautiful bed. It was unlike the pallets (the straw mattresses or makeshift beds) she was used to.[67]

Every night she prayed. "Oh, God, you know how much I am distressed, for I have told you again and again. Now, God, help me get my son. If you were in trouble, as I am, and I could help you, as you can me, think I wouldn't do it? Yes, God, you know I would do it.

"Oh, God, you know I have no money, but you can make the people do for me, and you must make the people do for me. I will never give you peace till you do, God.

"Oh, God, make the people hear me—don't let them turn me off, without hearing and helping me."[68]

Yet this was a time when there were many changes. The goal of the abolitionist movement was the immediate freedom of all slaves. Those trying to help former slaves worked so that all people would understand that slaves should be treated equally. But although there were some people who believed in this movement, there were many people who still didn't. They didn't want to help. They didn't want to see changes happening.

Isabella's prayers were answered, for even though she was a former slave, she found supporters of the abolitionist movement: clerks, lawyers, judges, and others who listened with respect. Many even helped where they could. These helpers also believed that slavery should be abolished.

Isabella persisted in asking for help and she finally made it to court. When her case was heard, she was the first black woman to win a case against a white man. Her son was returned to her. Isabella's heart ached to see him, for he had surely faced many hard times as a slave in the South. But because of his mother's persistence, Peter was back in her care.

In 1843, Isabella changed her name to Sojourner Truth. A sojourner is a wanderer. Isabella knew she had a mission to travel and to share the truth about slavery and the need for equality for all people. From that day forward "Sojourner Truth" set out to travel and preach. She gave numerous abolitionist speeches, and during the Civil War she helped recruit black troops for the Union Army.

Soon Sojourner was a powerful voice fighting against slavery. Sojourner's prayers were answered—not only for her son, but also for many others. With her help and voice, slavery was eventually abolished, and history was forever changed.

Faith in God will give you courage to continue on

Sojourner Truth wanted freedom for her son, and she was determined to get it. Yet her determination didn't come from her resources. It came from trusting God and knowing what he could do. Sojourner prayed again and again for her son. She asked that the Lord lead her to the right people, and she didn't stop asking until her prayer was answered.

Hebrews 11:1 says, "Now faith is the substance of things hoped for, the evidence of things not seen" (KJV). Sojourner couldn't see how her son's freedom could come about, but she kept praying and trusting that it would happen.

Sometimes in life our problems seem too big for us. Yet we can have faith that God can do what we cannot. His job is to handle the problems. Our job is to keep praying.

Something to Think About

Do you have a problem that seems difficult to solve? Have you prayed about it? What can you do to commit yourself to pray more and more? How do answered prayers encourage us to pray?

In Her Own Words

Do you ever feel small and alone? Do you feel like no one is paying attention to your needs? Sojourner felt that way. Yet as she prayed, she realized that someone was paying attention ... God.

> Oh! how little did I feel ... Neither would you wonder, if you could have seen me, in my ignorance and destitution, trotting about the streets, meanly clad, bare-headed, and bare-footed! Oh, God only could have made such people hear me; and he did it in answer to my prayers.[69]

Sojourner knew that she had little to offer. She owned nothing and had no material importance, but she had a big

God. And she struggled forward, believing in God, until the victory was won.

How She Changed History

Sojourner Truth gave speeches about slavery. She spoke with passion about the horrible treatment of many slaves. Sojourner believed strongly that all human beings should be treated with care and respect. She also shared in speeches that women should be treated the same as men and not as less important people (which was also a problem in Sojourner's time).

Sojourner's care for those forgotten or abused by others also caused her to speak out about the relocation of Southern slaves to new places where they could live in freedom. People listened and paid attention. New laws were passed and those who once were burdened by slavery and oppression gained new freedoms.

It's in the Bible

God led Abraham to the Promised Land, and Lot went along with him. When Abraham and Lot's flocks became too large to split the same property, the men split up, and Lot chose to move to the city of Sodom.

Sodom was a wicked city at the time. There was nothing good happening there. Through a visitor, God told Abraham that he was going to destroy Sodom. Abraham was upset because his nephew Lot lived there. Abraham cared for those who would be lost, and just like Sojourner Truth, he pleaded with God again and again and again.

Abraham approached him and said, "Will you sweep away both the righteous and the wicked? Suppose you find fifty righteous people living there in the city—will you still sweep it away and not spare it for their sakes? Surely you wouldn't do such a thing, destroying the righteous along with the wicked. Why, you would be treating the righteous and the wicked exactly the same! Surely you wouldn't do that! Should not the Judge of all the earth do what is right?"

And the LORD replied, "If I find fifty righteous people in Sodom, I will spare the entire city for their sake."

—Genesis 18:23–26 (NLT)

Next, Abraham asked if God would save the city if there were only forty-five, then forty, then thirty, then twenty, then ten. Each time the Lord said that he would be gracious.

Finally, Abraham said, "Lord, please don't be angry with me if I speak one more time. Suppose only ten are found there?"

And the LORD replied, "Then I will not destroy it for the sake of the ten."

When the LORD had finished his conversation with Abraham, he went on his way, and Abraham returned to his tent.   *—Genesis 18:32–33 (NLT)*

Abraham pleaded for the people. Instead of getting upset at Abraham, God listened. He knew Abraham's heart.

In the end, there weren't even ten godly people in the city, and the city was destroyed. Yet even though the city was lost, Abraham's prayers made a difference, Genesis 19:29 says, "But God had listened to Abraham's request and kept Lot safe, removing him from the disaster that engulfed the cities on the plain" (NLT).

If we pray with compassion, faith, and persistence, our prayers will make a difference. Sometimes the prayers aren't answered in the exact way we like, but God does hear us. And often, because of our prayers, the lives of others are forever changed.

Your Life

Sometimes God asks us to speak up for those who cannot speak up for themselves. Do you know someone who is being bullied? Do you know someone who needs a friend to speak out for him or her? Pray for that person. Also pray and ask God to help you to stand up for truth. Finally, seek caring adults to help you with your cause. Sojourner didn't do the work alone. Instead, she gathered others to join her cause.

Our prayers can save others.

CHAPTER 14

CATHERINE BOOTH

Prayers for God to Raise an Army

When She Lived:
1829 – 1890 AD

→ **1847 AD**

One woman's desire to bring salvation to a few raises up an army

The breeze of the English countryside carried the sounds of life through the bedroom window, but young Catherine Mumford lay in a bed. Her body ached, and there were many days she questioned why God had allowed her pain. A spinal curvature forced her to stay in bed for months at a time.[70] Catherine could not go out with friends. By the time she was 12 years old, she'd read the Bible eight times. She was young, but she felt very old. Laying there for hours at a time, Catherine came to realize the importance of salvation from a personal relationship with Jesus Christ—not only for her, but for others.

She was especially concerned about her father, who did not have a personal relationship with Jesus Christ. The seeds of prayers for her father took root and grew. Soon Catherine's heart was filled with a longing for all those she met to know and trust Jesus Christ.

In 1844, when her family moved to Brixton, she and her mother joined a chapel. For three years, Catherine Mumford taught a senior Sunday school class of fifteen girls. It was then that a desire for public ministry stirred within her.

Catherine married William Booth in 1850. A young preacher, William was growing in popularity, yet Catherine and William did not agree on everything. Catherine believed that women should be allowed to preach. And William said, "I would not stop a woman preaching on any account." But he added that neither would he "encourage one to begin."[71]

While she believed women should be able to preach, Catherine was too scared to try it herself. But everything changed one day in the Gateshead Bethesda Chapel. As Catherine sat there, a strange compulsion seized her, and she felt she must rise and speak. Still, a battle waged inside her.

You will look like a fool and have nothing to say, an inner voice taunted her. Catherine decided it was the devil's voice.

That's just the point, she responded in her mind. *I have never yet been willing to be a fool for Christ. Now I will be one.*[72]

Catherine rose and spoke. Her husband William was so

impressed that over time he accepted and encouraged his wife to pursue preaching.

In 1864, William and Catherine joined forces and started the Christian Mission, which later became the Salvation Army. They held great revival services, yet not everyone appreciated their work. Many times, they were imprisoned for preaching in the open air.

This did not stop Catherine's work and preaching. "I know not what he is about to do with me," Catherine said, "but I have given myself entirely into his hands."[73]

Catherine did more than just preach. She organized Food-for-the-Million Shops where the poor could buy hot soup and a three-course dinner for a sixpence (which was a small amount of money). On special occasions, such as Christmas Day, she would cook over 300 dinners to be distributed to the poor of London. At the same time, the Salvation Army was reaching people that the Church of England was failing to reach. In 1882, a survey of London found out that on one weeknight there were 17,000 people worshipping with the Salvation Army, compared to 11,000 in ordinary churches.[74]

While Catherine worked tirelessly to help women working in horrible conditions, she also raised eight children of her own, all of whom were active in the Salvation Army.[75]

Catherine's last words were, "The waters are rising, but so am I. I am not going under but over. Do not be concerned about dying; go on living well, the dying will be right." And the prayers that started with praying for her father—praying for courage and zeal—forever changed her. More than that, history was forever changed.

When we pray for boldness to reach one soul, God might give us the boldness to reach many

The more time Catherine spent reading God's Word, the more concerned she became over the souls of people, starting with her father. In most families, there are those who follow God and those who don't. Even young children can pray for those in their family to come to know Jesus. As their prayers continue, they can pray with diligence for those outside their family too.

Something to Think About

Who is someone in your family who needs to accept the free gift of God's salvation? How can you pray? Whom can you ask to pray with you?

In Her Own Words

Catherine was raised by a godly mother, but her father was not a follower of Jesus. This is a note she wrote in her journal as a teen:

> I was much blessed in the morning at private prayer, particularly in commending my dear parents into the hands of God. I sometimes get into an agony of feeling while praying for my dear father. O my Lord, answer prayer, and bring him back to Thyself! Never let that tongue, which once delighted in praising Thee, and in showing others Thy willingness to save, be engaged in uttering the lamentations of the lost! O awful thought! Lord, have mercy! Save him, in any

> way Thou seest best, though it be ever so painful. If by removing me Thou canst do this, cut short Thy work and take me home. Let me be bold to speak in Thy name. Oh, give me true Christian courage and lively zeal, and when I write to him from this place, bless what I say to the good of his soul!

In a later entry she adds:

> I received a letter from my dear father, which did me good telling me of some resolutions he had half formed. I have written a long letter to him, and feel much blessed in so doing. I believe I had the assistance of the Spirit.[76]

How She Changed History

Catherine Booth never intended to make people more open and accepting of women preachers, but that's what she did. She also encouraged women to take a more active role by helping and serving in their communities. During Catherine's time, women were seen as second class citizens. Catherine's preaching and work showed people that women could help the public in many ways. Catherine Booth is remembered for starting the Salvation Army. She is also remembered as someone who fought for women and children to have a voice in their communities. As a follower of God, Catherine knew men, women, and children were all important in God's eyes.

It's in the Bible

Sometimes we think we have to be bold when praying or preaching alone. We feel as if we have to pull out our inner strength and make ourselves be braver. This isn't true.

Peter and John were two of Jesus' closest friends, and they still had times when they were afraid of praying for others or telling people about Jesus. Instead of hiding, or instead of listening to the negative voice of the devil, they prayed and asked God to give them boldness and power.

"And now, O Lord, hear their threats, and give us, your servants, great boldness in preaching your word. Stretch out your hand with healing power; may miraculous signs and wonders be done through the name of your holy servant Jesus."

After this prayer, the meeting place shook, and they were all filled with the Holy Spirit. Then they preached the word of God with boldness.

—Acts 4:29–31 (NLT)

God answered the prayer of Peter and John by giving them the Holy Spirit. God's Spirit is available to you if you ask. He will help you pray for others and share the news about him with boldness.

Your Life

Do you need boldness to share Jesus with others? Maybe God wants to use you to raise up a spiritual army too. And know that if God asks you to build an army, he'll also give you his Holy Spirit to do his work.

Pray for boldness to reach one, and God might lead you to reach many.

CHAPTER 15

DAVID LIVINGSTONE

One Story Inspires Many to Follow

When He Lived: 1813 – 1873 AD

→ **1853 AD**

David Livingstone inspires others to bring God's Word to the interior of Africa

David Livingstone scanned the horizon. The ocean and the land met in crashing waves. A new land where the Europeans had yet to cross. He'd made it. He was in South Africa.

David disembarked from this ship and took a deep breath of the salty air. Committing his life to Africa certainly wasn't the direction he'd expected to go when he was younger. Yet David was here because he'd given himself fully to God. His plans, he'd learned over the years, didn't matter as much as God's plans did.

David grew up in a poor home in Scotland. He was an avid reader, and by the age of nine he had memorized the longest chapter in the Bible, Psalm 119. When he was just 10 years old, David worked fourteen hours a day in a cotton spinning factory. He managed to read in the factory by placing his book on a spinning jenny. (A spinning jenny is a spinning wheel with many spindles. One worker was able to work eight or more spools at once, saving a lot of time.)

At age 12, David asked Jesus to forgive his sins. As grace washed over him, David knew salvation was the greatest need for all mankind. From that point, David decided he'd only take enough income to live on and give the rest to missions.

When he was in his twenties, David studied theology and medicine. He went to China first, but when those doors closed, he looked to South Africa. David heard of the need in Africa from London Missionary Society (LMS) missionary Robert Moffat. David met Robert in London when Robert was on leave from a missionary outpost in South Africa. Robert's words pierced David's heart.

"I've glimpsed at the smoke of a thousand villages, where no missionary has ever been," Robert said.[77]

Because of the dangers and unknowns of the continent, Europeans hadn't gone far inland. They stayed mostly on the coasts. In the interior of Africa, the rivers were dangerous. Deadly malaria plagued those who tried to venture inside. Whole expeditions had died because of that disease.

Travel was hard too. Forests, swamps, and hard terrain made it impossible to take wheeled transports inside. The only way in was to go by foot, and that's what David did.

David went forward without fear. He didn't fear the terrain. He didn't fear disease. He didn't even fear the tribespeople, including the Barka tribe who had murdered white fur traders.

He went forward, but even those in Africa didn't believe Livingstone could get to the interior — to those who had never heard of Jesus Christ.

"You never can cross that country to the tribes beyond; it is utterly impossible even for us Black men," said Chief Sechele, ruler of the Kwena people.[78]

David didn't listen. God had brought him to Africa. God would watch over each step, going into places that no European had gone before. As he continued on, he was not seen as a threat. Other expeditions had dozens of soldiers, armed with rifles and porters carrying supplies. The large number of men and guns made the locals feel worried and defensive. David did things differently. He traveled with just a few servants and porters. He bartered along the way. He soon was considered a friend by many.[79] Yet things weren't always easy.

David took his first missionary journey with his wife and children. His fourth child, Elizabeth, was born on the way. Two months after her birth, baby Elizabeth died and the rest of the family became sick. For a time, David sent his family home to London, but when David's wife joined him for the second journey, she too died of malaria. Yet David did not give up. He prayed harder.

David had lost too much, but he knew that his wife would want him to continue on. When she died, she had hope in heaven, but so many in Africa did not. Even though he was filled with sadness, David continued on. He knew he must do what he could to overcome the darkness and slavery found in Africa.

"I shall open up a path into the interior or perish. May He bless and make us blessings even unto death ... Shame upon us missionaries if we are to be outdone by slave traders!... If Christian missionaries and Christian merchants could remain throughout the year in the interior of the continent, in ten years, slave dealers will be driven out of the market."[80] David even believed he could go to where the slave traders couldn't go because he had God on his side.

In 1857, David published his book, *Missionary Travels and Researches in South Africa*. It quickly became a bestseller back at home. Through his travels, David opened Africa to all people. He also opened all peoples' hearts and minds to Africa. The concern and prayers of many traveled with him.

David Livingstone is known as "Africa's greatest missionary" even though he is recorded as having converted only one African: Sechele, who was the chief of the Kwena people of Botswana.[81] David did not have success in the way he expected—by many Africans coming to know Jesus Christ. Instead his dedication to the people of Africa made him a national hero. And several African Christian missionary programs were started. Many missionaries were inspired to follow in his footsteps, and these groups of people reached many more with the Good News of Jesus than David could have done on his own.

David Livingstone accomplished great things for African missions, yet at the end of his life, he didn't like to talk about all that had been done. Instead he spoke of what remained to be done before the gospel could be said to be preached to all nations.[82] Because of David Livingston, much of Africa heard the gospel of Jesus for the first time. More than that, thousands of fellow missionaries followed his example, and history was forever changed.

People need a chance to hear the Good News

There are people all over the world who have never heard about Jesus. What do they need most? Someone to tell them.

Romans 10:14 says, "But how can they call on him to save them unless they believe in him? And how can they believe in him if they have never heard about him? And how can they hear about him unless someone tells them?" (NLT).

As a young boy, David Livingstone wanted to make a difference by giving to missions. Then God did something in his heart, and David became a missionary.

As he went, David prayed that God would open the interior of Africa to him. The interior was open, and David remained there until his death. Even as an old man, David continued to commit himself to God's use. Even though David's work didn't look successful, since he had just one convert, God used David until the very end by inspiring other missionaries. He passed away on his knees, praying for all those who still needed to hear the good news about Jesus. And history was forever changed.

Something to Think About

How do you want to make a difference? What are you praying for? What about David Livingstone inspires you?

In His Own Words

David Livingstone kept a journal his whole life. Here is what he wrote on his sixtieth birthday. He was still in Africa all those years later.

> 19 March 1872 – Birthday. My Jesus, my King, my life, my All; I again dedicate my whole self to Thee. Accept me and grant, O gracious Father, that ere this year is gone I may finish my task. In Jesus; name I ask it. Amen, so let it be. David Livingstone.[83]
>
> *David Livingstone*

On May 1, 1873, Livingstone was found dead, kneeling at his bedside, apparently in prayer.

How He Changed History

David Livingstone is considered one of the greatest European missionary explorers of Africa. He entered the interior of Africa to share the Good News of Jesus, and he inspired many others to follow. But David Livingstone wasn't only known for his missionary work, he also called for a worldwide crusade to defeat the slave trade. The way to liberate Africa, he believed, was to introduce the "three C's": commerce, Christianity, and civilization. His written and oral messages contributed to the "Scramble for Africa." David Livingston could only accomplish so much on the African soil, but his passion to reach the African people led to a movement that impacted a continent.

it's in the Bible

Did you know that God has always had a heart for Africa? Long before David Livingstone walked the earth, God made a way for an important official from Africa to hear the good news of Jesus.

It all started when Jesus' disciple Philip heard an Ethiopian believer reading from the book of Isaiah. Philip helped the Ethiopian understand that the Scriptures were fulfilled through Jesus. Then something amazing happened.

> As for Philip, an angel of the Lord said to him, "Go south down the desert road that runs from Jerusalem to Gaza." So he started out, and he met the treasurer of Ethiopia, a eunuch of great authority under the Kandake, the queen of Ethiopia. The eunuch had gone to Jerusalem to worship, and he was now returning. Seated in his carriage, he was reading aloud from the book of the prophet Isaiah.   —Acts 8:26–28 (NLT)

With the leading of the Holy Spirit, Philip went over and talked to the man. He helped the man understand a passage from Isaiah.

> The passage of Scripture he had been reading was this:
> "He was led like a sheep to the slaughter.
> And as a lamb is silent before the shearers,
> He did not open his mouth.
> He was humiliated and received no justice.
> Who can speak of his descendants?
> For his life was taken from the earth."
> The eunuch asked Philip, "Tell me, was the prophet talking about himself or someone else?" So beginning with this same Scripture, Philip told him the Good News about Jesus.   —Acts 8:32–35 (NLT)

God led Philip to share the Good News of Jesus with the Ethiopian. Because of what Philip shared, the man became a believer and asked to be baptized.

God led David Livingstone to share the Good News of Jesus with other Africans that no one else had been able to reach. God wants all people around the world to know about him. It's amazing that God also uses ordinary people to reach others for him.

Your Life

During your life, God may call you to do something that others think is impossible. The good news is that if God asks you to go out for him, he's certain to go with you. We don't need to think of dangerous things to do for God. Instead we simply need to seek to love and obey him. As we love him and obey him, Jesus will show us who we need to share his Good News with. It might be in Africa, or it might be next door.

As you seek him and pray to Him, God will reveal his good and right plans for you.

God wants all people to hear his Word.

CHAPTER 16

FLORENCE NIGHTINGALE

A Prayer for Practical Usefulness

When She Lived: 1820 – 1910 AD

→ 1854 AD

God uses one young woman to change nursing practices around the world

Florence was not a common name for a girl in 1820, but Florence Nightingale was given that name because that's where she was born, in Florence, Italy, while her parents were traveling. Florence was raised in a church-going family, and an entry in her diary shortly before her seventeenth birthday reads: "On February 7th, 1837, God spoke to me and called me to his service."[84]

For many years, Florence didn't know what that calling was. She was concerned that being married would make it hard to follow God, so she turned down a marriage proposal from a man she loved.

In the spring of 1844, she came to believe her calling was to be a nurse, but her family opposed it. At the time, nursing was not a suitable profession. Nurses were known to be largely unskilled and uneducated, and to often drink too much alcohol. Nursing was also a messy job; it was a common practice not to wash or change bed sheets, even after a patient died in his bed.

Florence was finally allowed to go into training, and she went to Kaiserswerth, Germany, to learn and train with the Lutheran order of Deaconesses, who were running a hospital there.

Back in London, Florence's family connections helped her to become the supervisor of a sanatorium in London. The place hadn't been managed well and the patients weren't well cared for. Soon, the horrible place was transformed into a model hospital.[85]

In 1854, war came to the Crimea (in Russia, on the north edge of the Black Sea). British soldiers were fighting, and Florence obtained permission to lead a group of thirty-eight nurses there. She helped organize the hospitals, created a system where injured soldiers could send home money to their families, improved the sanitation, and set up reading rooms with writing tables for the men to write home. At night, she would patrol the halls, walking with a dim lamp. Florence wanted to ensure that all was well, and she was famously called "the Lady with the Lamp."

In April 1856, when the war was over, Florence returned to England a national hero. Not wanting all the attention, she hid away in a convent and spent her days in prayer.

When she finally emerged, Florence lobbied Parliament for suitable legislation to overhaul nursing and basic medical care. She wrote pamphlets informing the country that the main cause of deaths in the Army wasn't from wounds, but from infection.

Florence wasn't without fault. For many years, she struggled with her faith and the church, especially the way it tried to stand between individuals and God. Finally she felt the Lord's voice stirring in her heart. He said to her, "You are here to carry out my program. I am not here to carry out yours."[86]

In 1859, Florence wrote the book *Notes on Nursing*, which became the foundation of many nursing schools. God, indeed, used Florence in her role as a nurse, transforming nursing practices for a generation. She is so respected for her work that a Nightingale Pledge was created to honor her. It has been revised many times, but this is how it originally read:

> I solemnly pledge myself before God and in the presence of this assembly to pass my life in purity and to practise my profession faithfully.
>
> I shall abstain from whatever is deleterious and mischievous, and shall not take or knowingly administer any harmful drug.
>
> I shall do all in my power to maintain and elevate the standard of my profession and will hold in confidence all personal matters committed to my keeping and all family affairs coming to my knowledge in the practice of my calling.

> I shall be loyal to my work and devoted towards
> the welfare of those committed to my care.[87]

Sometimes we need to accept God's call, even when we don't know how we are to serve

Florence Nightingale was only sixteen years old when she was called by God. She did not know what he asked of her, but she did know he was asking. She had no idea how he would use her to transform nursing practices of the day, but still she was willing to follow his call.

First Corinthians 1:26–27 says, "Brothers and sisters, think of what you were when you were called. Not many of you were wise by human standards; not many were influential; not many were of noble birth. But God chose the foolish things of the world to shame the wise; God chose the weak things of the world to shame the strong."

Never doubt what one person can do with God's strength. Florence Nightingale was called years before she was capable of doing anything. Later, her passion and training helped her to make huge improvements in nursing. And history was forever changed.

Something to Think About

What things do you do well? Where do you feel weak? Do you think God will use your weaknesses or your strengths to make a difference? How can you turn to God to seek his strength?

In Her Own Words

In 1850, Florence's family sent her on a tour of Egypt for her health. Some extracts from her diary follow:

> March 7. God called me in the morning and asked me would I do good for Him, for Him alone without the reputation.
>
> March 9. During half an hour I had by myself in my cabin, settled the question with God.
>
> April 1. Not able to go out but wished God to have it all His own way. I like Him to do exactly as He likes without even telling me the reason.
>
> May 12. Today I am thirty – the age Christ began his mission. No more childish things. No more love. No more marriage. Now Lord let me think only of Thy Will, what Thou willest me to do. Oh Lord Thy Will, Thy Will.[88]
>
> *Florence Nightingale*

How She Changed History

Florence Nightingale is the "mother of modern nursing." This means that so many of the practices that we use today were birthed from the changes she brought about. Because of Florence, nurses know better how to care for patients. Florence taught the nurses she worked with how to tend to the ill with cleanliness and also with compassion. In 1870, Florence mentored an American nurse, Linda Richards, who returned to the United States and established the first high quality nursing school in America.[89] International Nursing Day is celebrated around the world on Florence Nightingale's birthday. Because of her willingness to commit her life to God's service, nursing was transformed, saving millions of lives.

it's in the Bible

Sometimes in the Bible, God let people know the task he destined for them. For example, God told Moses he would lead the children of Israel out of Egypt. But most of the time, God's directions aren't so clear, like in the excerpt with Abraham below.

> The LORD had said to Abram, "Leave your native country, your relatives, and your father's family, and go to the land that I will show you. I will make you into a great nation. I will bless you and make you famous, and you will be a blessing to others. I will bless those who bless you and curse those who treat you with contempt. All the families on earth will be blessed through you."
>
> So Abram departed as the LORD had instructed, and Lot went with him. Abram was seventy-five years old when he left Haran. He took his wife, Sarai, his nephew Lot, and all his wealth—his livestock and all the people he had taken into his household at Haran—and headed for the land of Canaan. When they arrived in Canaan, Abram traveled through the land as far as Shechem. There he set up camp beside the oak of Moreh. At that time, the area was inhabited by Canaanites.
>
> Then the LORD appeared to Abram and said, "I will

give this land to your descendants." And Abram built an altar there and dedicated it to the LORD, who had appeared to him. After that, Abram traveled south and set up camp in the hill country, with Bethel to the west and Ai to the east. There he built another altar and dedicated it to the LORD, and he worshiped the LORD. Then Abram continued traveling south by stages toward the Negev.

—*Genesis 12:1–9 (NLT)*

The most important thing about following God is being willing to be led by him. Sometimes we need to accept God's call, even when we don't know where we are going. But when we follow God, we can make a huge difference in the world.

Your Life

God needs loyal and devoted people to care for others in many ways. He used Florence Nightingale to impact nursing. You never know how he'll use you. You can be the person to make a huge discovery, bringing positive changes to generations. Today, pray that God will use you in whatever way he sees fit.

One person can make a huge difference in the world with God's help.

CHAPTER 17

GEORGE MÜLLER

Bold in Faith

When He Lived: 1805 – 1898

→ **1877 AD**

George Müller prays for things, big and small

George Müller stood at the bow of the ship. He was headed to Quebec, but the ship had hardly moved. A thick fog surrounded them, making progress impossible.

It was a cool August day. George knew the number of days still left in their voyage. He also knew that at this rate he wasn't going to make his schedule. Twenty-four hours had passed since they'd come to a standstill. George approached the bridge to talk to the captain.

The captain glanced up at George as he entered. Weariness creased his face. "Captain, I have come to tell you that you must be in Quebec on Saturday afternoon."

The captain slowly shook his head. "It is impossible."

George straightened his stance. "Then very well, if your ship cannot take me, God will find some other way. I have never broken an engagement in fifty-seven years; let us go down into the chart room and pray."

The captain glanced over at George as if he'd lost his mind, but George knew that prayer wasn't just a nice idea. It was *the* answer to their dilemma.

"Do you know how dense this fog is?" the captain finally asked.

"No," George replied. "My eye is not on the density of the fog, but on the living God who controls every circumstance of my life."

George knelt down and prayed simply, asking God to lift the fog. He finished, and the captain opened his mouth, but George put a hand on his shoulder. "As you do not believe he will answer. And as I believe he has. There is no need whatever for you to pray about it."[90]

The captain's eyes widened. George offered him a smile. "Captain, I have known the Lord for fifty-seven years and there has never been a single day when I have failed to get an audience with the King. Get up, Captain, and open the door and you will find the fog has gone." There was no wavering in his voice. George spoke with commitment. God had answered numerous prayers—thousands and thousands that George had recorded over the years.

The captain rose. With tentative steps he opened the door. A warm breeze blew in, but the fog was gone. George Müller also knew with confidence that he'd make it on time to his promised engagement. Not only that, Captain Dutton found faith in God. Captain Dutton retold the story many times as master of the ship the *Sardinian*.

George Müller's strong faith hadn't just appeared overnight. Instead, George's faith grew as he prayed. He witnessed God answering again and again and again.[91] George learned to pray for everything—big things and small things alike.

Most of George's prayers centered on the orphans that he cared for. The orphanages he established covered thirteen acres of ground on Ashley Downs in Bristol, England.[92] George felt God stirring his heart and asking him to build these orphanages, but at the time George only had two shillings (50 cents) in his pocket. George never approached others for money asking them to support the cause. Instead, he turned to God, reminding God that these were his orphans. God was the Father to the fatherless. It was God's work.

George never asked any man for money, but over $7 million was sent to him for building the orphan homes and caring for the children. At the time of George's death, the orphanages cared for 2,000 children. And during that time they never missed setting a meal before the children, not once.

George was not raised knowing God. Growing up in Germany he used to steal money from his father. As a teenager, he snuck out of a hotel twice without paying for the room. One of the times he was caught and taken to jail.

George went to Bible college, but that didn't mean he loved God or the Bible. He loved going to bars, drinking, partying, and gambling. One day, when George was in college, a friend invited him to a Bible study. George went so he could make fun of the Christians, but it turned out he liked the study! He saw people who knew and loved God, and he liked what he saw. By the end of the week George knelt at his bed and asked God to forgive his sins.[93]

The first prayer of forgiveness led to many, many prayers being answered. Prayers such as the one on the ship. Or prayers for the orphans. In his lifetime, George Müller personally recorded over 50,000 specific prayers that were answered.[94] Because of this, thousands of people have followed his example of faith in prayer — and history was forever changed.

God hears the prayers we pray

1 John 5:14 says, "This is the confidence we have in approaching God: that if we ask anything according to his will, he hears us."

George Müller is an example of this. In his lifetime, George Müller cared for 10,024 orphans. He established 117 schools, which offered Christian education to over 120,000 children, many of them orphans.[95] George never made requests for financial support, nor did he go into debt. Many times, he received unsolicited food donations only hours before they were needed to feed the children, further strengthening his faith in God.

For example, on one occasion there was no food in the house, yet George asked the children to sit at the table and give thanks for breakfast. As they finished praying, the baker knocked at the door with enough bread for them all. Then the milkman stopped by with fresh milk because his cart broke down in front of the orphanage.[96]

George Müller wasn't afraid to pray, and because of that his prayers were answered! Can you imagine what would happen if all of us decided to pray like George Müller?

When it comes to prayer, there is no telling how your life history—and the history of those around you, can forever change.

Something to Think About

Are you ever afraid to pray? Why? What would have happened if George Müller had been too afraid to pray? Why does God want us to pray boldly?

In His Own Words

George Müller is known as someone who didn't give up. He knew that if something was good, and for the glory of God, it was something to pray about. "I live in the spirit of prayer. I pray as I walk about, when I lie down and when I rise up. And the answers are always coming. Thousands and tens of thousands of times have my prayers been answered. When once I am persuaded that a thing is right and for the glory of God, I go on praying for it until the answer comes. George Müller never gives up!"[97]

How He Changed History

When George Müller moved to Bristol with his wife and son, the city had poor sanitation. The dirty water spread cholera, and hundreds of people died. Children lost their parents and became orphans. They begged on the streets in order to survive. The Müllers opened their first Orphan House on April 11, 1836. More homes were opened through the years, and

George Müller oversaw the work until his death. Even after his death, the work of caring for orphans continued for 100 years. During that time, almost 18,000 orphans were cared for.[98]

George's caring and housing of orphans changed the children's lives, and it also impacted how orphans were viewed by their community. Most people saw orphans as bothersome and a pest on society, but George's belief was that these children could be raised to be godly men and women and good citizens. His staff cared for their souls just as they cared for the children's bodies.

The condition of orphans in nearby London was brought to light in the novel *Oliver Twist* by Charles Dickens. It was published in 1837, the year after George's first orphanage opened. This novel helped promote the need for George's work, and society's view of orphans changed.[99]

it's in the Bible

In the Bible there was another man who was bold in his faith. Elijah knew that God was big enough to handle his requests, especially in front of those who refused to believe.

In 1 Kings 18:25–26, Elijah challenged the prophets of Baal to a test. He set up an altar for God and asked 450 false prophets to do the same for Baal. The test was that fire would light the altar of the true God.

Even though the false prophets danced and shouted all day, nothing happened on the altar to Baal. Yet when Elijah prayed, fire fell, burning up the sacrifice, alter, wood, and water that Elijah poured over the altar.

Elijah called to the people, "Come over here!" They all crowded around him as he repaired the altar of the LORD that had been torn down. He took twelve stones, one to represent each of the tribes of Israel, and he used the stones to rebuild the altar in the name of the LORD. Then he dug a trench around the altar large enough to hold about three gallons. He piled wood on the altar, cut the bull into pieces, and laid the pieces on the wood.

Then he said, "Fill four large jars with water, and pour the water over the offering and the wood."

After they had done this, he said, "Do the same thing again!" And when they were finished, he said, "Now do it a third time!" So they did as he said, and the water ran around the altar and even filled the trench.

At the usual time for offering the evening sacrifice, Elijah the prophet walked up to the altar and prayed, "O LORD, God of Abraham, Isaac, and Jacob, prove today that you are God in Israel and that I am your servant. Prove that I have done all this at your command. O LORD, answer me! Answer me so these people will know that you, O LORD, are God and that you have brought them back to yourself."

Immediately the fire of the LORD flashed down from heaven and burned up the young bull, the wood, the stones, and the dust. It even licked up all the water in the trench! And when all the people saw it, they fell face down on the ground and cried out, "The LORD—he is God! Yes, the LORD is God!"

—1 Kings 18:30–39 (NLT)

Elijah knew who his God was. He knew what his God could do. Elijah prayed bold prayers and it showed all those present that the Lord was God indeed!

Your Life

God is looking for people who will pray boldly about things both big and small. Both Elijah and George Müller looked to God rather than the circumstances around them. The more you pray, the more God has the opportunity to act. The more God acts, the greater your faith for continued prayers. Praying, and seeing God answer, is the best faith builder there is!

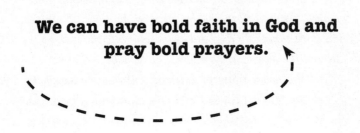

We can have bold faith in God and pray bold prayers.

CHAPTER 18

BILLY SUNDAY

Crazy Prayers

When He Lived: 1862 – 1935 AD

→ **1886 AD**

Billy Sunday: from athlete to evangelist

Billy Sunday stood in right field during a Chicago White Sox game. He considered the men on the field his closest friends. Mike Kelley was catching and John G. Clarkson was pitching.

Their opponents had two men out, a man on second, and one on third. There were three balls and two strikes. The game rested on the next play.

"One more and we got 'em!" Billy called. Billy was a player in the National League. Though he was born into poverty and had grown up an orphan, Billy had finally made a name for himself. He hunkered down to watch the next pitch.

Charley, the man at bat, loved low balls. Billy guessed

that Clarkson would pitch high. Yet when Clarkson threw the pitch, his foot slipped and the ball went low. Charley swung hard, and cracked the ball. It rose. Billy could tell it was going long, far over his head.

Billy turned and ran, and as he ran he prayed. "God, if you ever helped mortal man, help me to get that ball, and you haven't very much time to make up your mind, either."[100]

Billy ran and jumped over the bench. He thought he was close enough to catch the ball, but when he looked back, it was still high over his head. Holding his breath, Billy jumped and shoved out his left hand. The ball hit it and stuck!

The ball landed solid, but Billy's body kept moving. He sailed beyond the field as his momentum carried him. Billy fell under a team of horses and then rolled out of their way. With gusto, he jumped up, waving the ball in his hand.

Billy's great catch was an answer to a crazy prayer. The prayer was important, not because Billy caught the ball, but because it was a glimpse of the changes happening inside him.

Just the night before this big game, Billy had accepted Jesus Christ. It was an ordinary Sunday afternoon, and he'd gone drinking with fellow ball players. He and the others sat at the corner of a vacant lot. Across the street, men and women were playing instruments and singing gospel hymns. The hymns reminded Billy of the songs his mother used to sing in church.

As Billy sat there, he thought of Sunday school and the love of those people he used to know. Many were now gone from this earth.

Emotion filled Billy's chest, and sobs erupted. They didn't stop.

One of the men approached him. "We are going to the Pacific Garden Mission. Won't you come down to the mission? I am sure you will enjoy it. You can hear drunkards tell how they have been reformed and girls tell how they have been saved from the red light district."

Billy rose and said to the boys, "I'm through. I am going to Jesus Christ. We've come to the parting of the ways."[101] After that, Billy was a changed man.

Billy Sunday gave his life to Jesus Christ that day. He played baseball until 1891. That year, he turned down a baseball contract for $3,500 a year to accept a position with the Chicago YMCA at $83 a month. His job title was Assistant Secretary, but Billy used it as a chance to tell people about Jesus. He visited the sick, talked to troubled people, and went to saloons to invite folks to evangelistic meetings.[102]

In 1893, Billy became the assistant to a well-known evangelist, and by 1896, Billy set off on his own, mostly in Iowa and Illinois. Some thought he should have stayed a ball player, though his fame helped draw people to hear him share the gospel. Billy had been on his way to being a star when he found Jesus. He excelled as a base runner, able to make the trip around the bases in fourteen seconds, but he excelled even more at giving a dramatic message to his listeners.

Billy had a flair for his talks, just as he had a flair for baseball. He spoke in street talk and used a lot of body language. Billy made people laugh, and then he belted them with the gospel.

The great catch on the ball field may have been his first answered prayer, but it wasn't his last. Billy's salvation not only changed his life, but it also changed his career. Billy preached whenever he was given the chance. He preached more than 20,000 sermons to more than one hundred million people. Many people discovered Jesus' forgiveness for their sins because of Billy's passionate messages, and history was forever changed.

People who share the love of God draw more people to him

Billy Sunday had been living for himself. Even though he had fame and money, he was not happy. Men and women singing gospel hymns reminded Billy of people he once knew—people who had shared the love of Christ with him when he was a young boy.

Those memories of love made Billy realize how empty his life was. Those hymn-singers brought the promise of Christ to a hurting soul.

Second Corinthians 2:14–17 says, "But thanks be to God, who always leads us as captives in Christ's triumphal procession and uses us to spread the aroma of the knowledge of him everywhere. For we are to God the pleasing aroma of Christ among those who are being saved and those who are perishing. To one we are an aroma that brings death; to the other, an aroma that brings life. And who is equal to such a task? Unlike so many, we do not peddle the word of God for profit. On the contrary, in Christ we speak before God with sincerity, as those sent from God."

The knowledge of Christ is spread through people. Billy's

friends thought those who were singing were foolish, but Billy saw the truth. He saw that they had the love he was missing. And their songs pointed Billy to God's perfect love.

Something to Think About

When was a turning point in your life? Which people in your life helped you to understand the love of God? Who is someone who needs to make a decision to accept Jesus as Lord? How can you pray for that person?

In His Own Words

In each of our lives there is a moment of decision. God will bring people to our lives who love him. We must decide if we love him too. We must decide if we will follow Jesus, or if we will go our own way. Billy had to make that decision one day. He made the right decision, and he never turned back. "I turned and left that little group on the corner of State and Madison streets and walked to the little mission and fell on my knees and staggered out of sin and into the arms of the Savior," Billy Sunday said.[103]

How He Changed History

Billy Sunday is known as a great preacher, but he also had major social influence in the temperance movement. The temperance movement was an organized effort to stop the excess drinking of alcohol. Alcohol was a huge problem during this era. Many people had drinking problems and they did not properly care for their families. The temperance movement led to Prohibition in 1919. This was an attempt to prohibit the consumption of alcohol.

Many people listened to Billy Sunday because of his famous background and his outspoken beliefs. He was welcomed into the homes of the upper class and honored by everyday citizens. One of Billy's most famous sermons was "Booze, or, Get on the Water Wagon." This sermon persuaded many to give up drinking.[104] His preaching almost certainly played a significant role in the adoption of the Eighteenth Amendment in 1919, which prohibited the manufacturing and drinking of alcohol.[105] And that is in addition to the thousands of lives that were transformed as they were also persuaded to turn to Christ for salvation.

it's in the Bible

Gideon lived in a time when Israel's enemies ruled over them. He lived in fear and worry, and he no doubt had seen a lot of destruction over the years.

It made no sense to Gideon when God sent a special messenger to him, an angel who said Gideon was supposed to lead Israel's army. Gideon felt weak, not strong. He wanted to make sure this message really was from God. Gideon wanted confidence that God would do what he said to save the Israelite army.

Just like Billy Sunday asked God to help him catch that ball, Gideon prayed a crazy prayer. When that was answered, he prayed another.

Soon afterward the armies of Midian, Amalek, and the people of the east formed an alliance against Israel

and crossed the Jordan, camping in the valley of Jezreel.
Then the Spirit of the LORD clothed Gideon with power.
He blew a ram's horn as a call to arms, and the men of
the clan of Abiezer came to him. He also sent messengers
throughout Manasseh, Asher, Zebulun, and Naphtali,
summoning their warriors, and all of them responded.

Then Gideon said to God, "If you are truly going to
use me to rescue Israel as you promised, prove it to me
in this way. I will put a wool fleece on the threshing floor
tonight. If the fleece is wet with dew in the morning but
the ground is dry, then I will know that you are going
to help me rescue Israel as you promised." And that is
just what happened. When Gideon got up early the next
morning, he squeezed the fleece and wrung out a whole
bowlful of water.

Then Gideon said to God, "Please don't be angry
with me, but let me make one more request. Let me use
the fleece for one more test. This time let the fleece remain
dry while the ground around it is wet with dew." So that
night God did as Gideon asked. The fleece was dry in the
morning, but the ground was covered with dew.

—Judges 6:33–40 (NLT)

Even though they were crazy prayers, God answered as
Gideon asked. Gideon's faith was built up, and, with God's
help, his army was victorious.

As we get to know God better, our prayers often change.
The better we know God, the more we trust him.

Your Life

Do the things you pray for sometimes seem crazy? You
don't have to worry if they do or not. God knows your

desires. He knows your heart. The important thing is that you pray.

Just because we pray doesn't mean God will always answer us how we ask. Sometimes he will. Sometimes he won't. It's not our job to worry about the answer. Our job is to go before God often and leave the rest up to him. Who knows, your crazy prayer just might be the launching point for God to do something amazing.

God listens to prayers— even crazy ones.

CHAPTER 19

HELEN KELLER

A Place for All

**When She Lived:
1880 – 1968 AD**

→ 1889 AD

Helen Keller showed the world that true love could overcome disabilities

The word came into Helen's life through her fingers: G-O-D. Yet even though the word was new, the concept was not. Though Helen Keller was both blind and deaf, she "saw" God in many ways. She felt him in the purr of a cat and in the warmth and the beating heart of a dog she loved. She had found him in the wings of a bird.

Helen Keller was born with all of her senses. But when she was 19 months old, she got sick with scarlet fever, an illness that left her both deaf and blind. After that, Helen did the best she could to communicate. She mainly communicated with Martha, the daughter of the family's cook, but by the time she was seven, Helen had come up with 60 signs that helped her communicate with her family.

In 1887, Helen's parents hired a teacher, Anne Sullivan. Anne taught Helen to communicate by spelling words using sign language signed into the palm of her hand. In 1888, Helen attended the Perkins Institute for the Blind. Around that time, Anne also introduced Helen to Bishop Phillips Brooks, who told her about Jesus.

"I always knew he was there," Helen responded, "but I didn't know his name!"[106]

Helen communicated with Bishop Brooks in letters. She asked him many questions about God and about her prayers to know God better.

> I wish to write about things I do not understand. Who made the earth and the seas, and everything? Who made the sun hot? Where was I before I came to mother? I know that plants grow from seeds which are in the ground, but I am sure people do not grow that way. I never saw a child-plant... Tell me something that Father Nature does. May I read the book called the Bible? Please tell your little pupil many things when you have much time.

In another letter she wrote,

> Why does the great Father in heaven think it is best for us to have very great sorrow and pain sometimes?... How did God tell people that his home was in heaven? When people do very wrong and hurt

animals and treat children unkindly God is grieved,
but what will he do to them to teach them to be pitiful
and loving? Please tell me something that you know
about God. I like so much to hear about my loving
Father, who is so good and wise.

Bishop Brooks was diligent in writing back, and a friendship began. Helen wrote to him again:

It fills my heart with joy to know that God loves me
so much that he wishes me to live always, and that
he gives me everything that makes me happy – loving
friends, a precious little sister, sweet flowers, and,
best of all, a heart that can love and sympathize and
a mind that can think and enjoy. I am thankful to
my heavenly Father for giving me all these precious
things … what is conscience? Once I wished very
much to read my new book about Heidi when teacher
had told me to study. Something whispered to me
that it would be wrong to disobey dear teacher. Was
it conscience that whispered to me it would be wrong
to disobey?

Bishop Brooks answered:

God tells us in our hearts that he is our Father.
That is what we call conscience – God's voice in our
hearts. Your heart takes God into it as the flower
takes in the sunshine; and then when you think God's

thoughts and do God's actions, it is a sign to you that God is in you and that you belong to him.

People have always thought that God must be their Father because he showed himself to them in the beautiful world, and because he spoke to them in their hearts' but he wanted to make it perfectly clear and sure to them, and so he came and lived among them. He took our human life and lived in it. He showed us what our life would be if it was absolutely filled with his spirit. That is what you read in the beautiful story of Jesus. And we can see him and hear what he says and come near to him, too; for we have the story of the precious words which he spoke and of how he was willing even to suffer to make men good; and we know that he promised when he went away that he would always be where people could talk to him and love him and tell him all their troubles and their needs.[107]

Many people know that Anne Sullivan is the one who taught Helen how to communicate with the world that she couldn't hear or see, but it was Bishop Brooks who taught her about the unseen world. Helen's prayers to know God were answered through a gentle bishop. And this foundation of truth stayed with Helen all her life.

Helen went on to graduate from Radcliffe College. She was the first deaf-blind person to earn a Bachelor of Arts degree. Determined to communicate with others, Helen learned to speak. She spent much of her life giving speeches and lectures. She also wrote twelve books. Helen spent most of her time traveling around the world, raising money for the blind.

As Helen grew older, her prayer was that all people— even those deaf and blind—should know God. Helen knew this was her personal calling. She felt she was under orders to do her part in sharing this message to her generation—and she succeeded.

Helen's lectures and fund-raising programs took her all over the world, and all over the world Helen shared the good news of Jesus Christ. Helen displayed what God could do through the life of a person with a disability, and history was forever changed.

God is in the unseen

Helen couldn't hear or see. And as a child, she couldn't communicate with the outside world except to share basic needs. Yet Helen knew there was a God. In her dark, quiet world, she sensed that he was there with her. She knew him, even though she couldn't ask about him. And when Helen was able to communicate, God was one of the first things she asked about.

We read about God's unseen qualities in Romans 1:20, "For since the creation of the world God's invisible qualities—his eternal power and divine nature—have been clearly seen, being understood from what has been made, so that people are without excuse."

God's nature is seen and felt by everyone on earth— even though they do not ask. Thankfully, Helen had someone to ask questions of—Bishop Brooks. Through his responses, Helen was able to learn about the One she'd always known was there.

Something to Think About

In what ways do you see and feel God in the world around you? What questions do you have about God? Who can you ask about God? Who can you tell about God?

In Her Own Words

Helen couldn't see and she couldn't hear, and yet she was thankful. Maybe she was even more thankful for the ordinary daily things like warm sunshine and sweet-smelling flowers — things we often take for granted — because she didn't have her hearing or sight.

Helen once wrote:

> For three things I thank God every day of my life: thanks that he has vouchsafed me knowledge of his works; deep thanks that he has set in my darkness the lamp of faith; deep, deepest thanks that I have another life to look forward to — a life joyous with light and flowers and heavenly song.[108]
>
> *Helen Keller*

Not only did Helen thank God for this life and all she experienced, she also looked forward to the life to come. In heaven, Helen knew, she'd have a new, healed body, and she'd be able to hear and see amazing things.

How She Changed History

Helen Keller raised money for the
blind, and she also opened up schools
for the deaf and blind. Her efforts at the
first World Council for the Blind in 1931
helped make Braille the world standard.

She championed women's suffrage and child labor laws.
Overall, she changed public perception of what a disabled
person could accomplish.

It's in the Bible

For many years, and in many places, those with disabilities were looked down upon, but there is a biblical
story that reminds us that true love overlooks disabilities.

King David remembered his best friend Jonathan fondly.
Jonathan had died in a battle with the Philistines before
David was made king. David wondered if any of Jonathan's
family was still alive. He soon discovered that one of
Jonathan's sons, Mephibosheth, was alive. Mephibosheth
was crippled, but that didn't matter to David.

> "Don't be afraid!" David said. "I intend to show
> kindness to you because of my promise to your father,
> Jonathan. I will give you all the property that once be-
> longed to your grandfather Saul, and you will eat here
> with me at the king's table!"
>
> Mephibosheth bowed respectfully and exclaimed,
> "Who is your servant, that you should show such kind-
> ness to a dead dog like me?"
>
> Then the king summoned Saul's servant Ziba and
> said, "I have given your master's grandson everything
> that belonged to Saul and his family. You and your sons

and servants are to farm the land for him to produce food for your master's household. But Mephibosheth, your master's grandson, will eat here at my table." (Ziba had fifteen sons and twenty servants.)

Ziba replied, "Yes, my lord the king; I am your servant, and I will do all that you have commanded." And from that time on, Mephibosheth ate regularly at David's table, like one of the king's own sons.

Mephibosheth had a young son named Mica. From then on, all the members of Ziba's household were Mephibosheth's servants. And Mephibosheth, who was crippled in both feet, lived in Jerusalem and ate regularly at the king's table.   —*2 Samuel 9:7–13 (NLT)*

Even though Mephibosheth was disabled, David welcomed him. From that day forward, Mephibosheth had a place at the king's table. This is a glimpse into the heart of God.

Your Life

No matter what we have, how we look, or what we can (or can't) do, God loves us and welcomes us to his table. He asks that we care for and welcome others too.

Helen lived her life to help the blind community. Even though she had less than most of us, she gave deeply from her heart. She gave what God had given her: unconditional love. And all we can do is give the same.

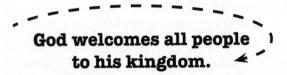

God welcomes all people to his kingdom.

CHAPTER 20

AMY CARMICHAEL

Standing in the Gap

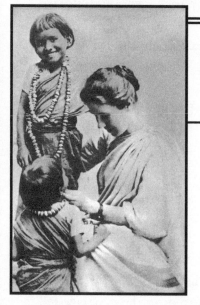

When She Lived:
1867 – 1951 AD

→ 1901 AD

Amy Carmichael helped the helpless with all her heart

Amy Carmichael's body ached as she sat in the chair. She'd been deep in prayer, but even then her body didn't stop hurting. Amy suffered from neuralgia, a disease of the nerves that made her whole body weak and achy. She was often in bed for weeks. Because of her condition, Amy didn't think she'd ever be a missionary, yet where she was weak God had been strong for her.

Prayer strengthened Amy. One day she gathered with friends in a Band Prayer meeting. The meeting was coming to a close when a woman rushed in.

"Oh, Amma! Amma! Do not pray! Your prayers are troubling me."

Amy looked at her in astonishment. Those in the room glanced at each other.

The excited woman was the birth mother of one of the young girls that Amy cared for. Amy was called Amma ("mother") by all the girls. Amy had rescued these young women from the Hindu temple. In the temple, horrible practices hurt young girls. Amy took them in and gave them a safe place to live.

The girls and young women were thankful for Amma's care and protection, but their parents wanted their children to continue in their traditional ways.

This one mother now stood before Amy. A devout Hindu, she grasped Amy's arm. Tears filled the woman's eyes. "Please, Amma, stop praying," the woman pleaded.

"When you went away last year I prayed. I prayed and prayed and prayed again to my god to dispel your work. For my daughter's heart was impressed with your words. I cried to my god to wash the words out. But has he washed them out? Oh no! And I prayed for a bridegroom for my daughter, and one came; and the cart was ready to take her away, and a hindrance occurred; so the marriage fell through. I wept till my eyes nearly dissolved. Another bridegroom came, and again an obstacle occurred. Later another bridegroom came, but the wedding was hindered by an obstacle. I cannot get my daughter married, the neighbors mock, and my caste is disgraced," cried the poor old mother, sobbing in her shame and confusion.

"Then I went to my god again and said, 'What more can I offer you? Have I not given you all I have? And you reject my prayer.' Then in a dream my (demon) god appeared, and he said, 'Tell the Christians not to pray, I can do nothing against their prayers. Their prayers are hindering me.' And so, I beseech you, stop your prayers for fourteen days—only fourteen days—till I get my daughter married."

"And after she is married?" Amy asked the mother.

"Oh, then she may freely follow your God." the mother declared, "I will hinder her no more."[109]

But Amy knew the proposed bridegroom came from three hundred miles away, with the idea to carry the poor girl off by force as soon as she was married. Amy and her friends had been praying night and day to God to hinder this marriage. And he was hindering.[110]

Amy and her friends weren't about to stop praying. Her whole life, it seemed, she had been taking care of young women.

Since her youth, Amy had given her whole life to God. Even before she was a missionary to India, she reached out to those whom much of the world rejected.

Growing up in Ireland, she had started a morning class for the "Shawlies," the mill girls who wore shawls instead of hats because that was all they could afford. Amy started a Sunday morning class for them, and it grew into a group of 500 young women.

Then Amy felt the call overseas. She first worked in Japan and then in Sri Lanka before going to Bangalore, India for her health. It was there she found her lifelong calling.[111]

In India, Amy learned about the plight of young girls. Her work started with a young girl named Preena. Preena had become a temple servant against her wishes but managed to escape. Amy started an organization and provided shelter for Preena. The shelter grew, and Amy cared for hundreds of young girls who came to her. Amy also stood against the threats of those who wanted the girls returned to the temple.

While living in India, Amy made sure that the children appreciated their culture. The rescued children had Indian names. Amy wore Indian dress and she even dyed her skin with dark coffee.

Known as "Amma" to thousands of children she rescued from the Hindu temple, Amy Carmichael spent fifty-three years in India, sharing the Gospel message of hope. She wrote many books and poems too. All of them shared her love and dedication to Christ and the young girls, his lambs, and history was forever changed.

Prayers and work can save others

In India, Amy saw that those who ran Hindu temples were hurting young women. Their evil practices had been going on for a long time. Amy could have said, "I am just one person, there isn't anything I can do." Yet, instead of saying that, Amy decided to do something. She decided to follow God's call.

Ephesians 2:10 says, "For we are God's masterpiece. He has created us anew in Christ Jesus, so we can do the good things he planned for us long ago" (NLT).

Amy prayed, and God showed her who she was to help. But Amy didn't stop praying then—prayer made her work possible. Prayer helped Amy discover the good work that God planned for her to do.

Something to Think About

In what ways do you like to help other people? What do you think God created you to do? How can God be strong when you are weak?

In Her Own Words

Amy cared for many, many people, but because of her illness she spent even more time resting and in prayer. She is a great example to us.

"Blessed are the single-hearted," she once said, "for they shall enjoy much peace. If you refuse to be hurried and pressed, if you stay your soul on God, nothing can keep you from that clearness of spirit which is life and peace. In that stillness you will know what His will is."[112]

Sometimes we get so busy hurrying about our lives that we miss spending time with God. But it is only as we spend time with God that we can discover his good plans.

How She Changed History

In India, Amy established a ministry to protect young girls who were sold as slaves and misused in Hindu temples. She showed courage and compassion and built an orphanage and school, but not everyone appreciated what she was doing.

Amy Carmichael lived in a time where missionaries were traveling all over the world, and some of these other missionaries thought that her work to shelter and protect the girls was taking away from the work of "saving souls."

Amy replied by saying, "Souls are more or less firmly attached to bodies."[113] Because of Amy's prayers and work, thousands of young girls were saved from bad situations. She also helped fellow missionaries to see that when one cares for the needs of people, they are then more interested in listening to biblical truth.

it's in the Bible

In life, there are people who stand up against wrong. That is what Amy Carmichael did. And, in the Bible, that is what a woman named Abigail did too.

Abigail was married to a man named Nabal. Nabal had a choice between helping and refusing to help. He made the wrong choice.

David (who later became King David) and hundreds of his fighting men traveled to the Desert of Moan. They were hungry and tired. Seeking help, David and his men journeyed to the household of a man named Nabal. They asked for food and drink. Nabal refused.

Because of Nabal's lack of hospitality and gratitude for their protection, David and his men planned on killing all the household of Nabal. Thankfully, Abigail stepped in.

> As she was riding her donkey into a mountain ravine, she saw David and his men coming toward her. David had just been saying, "A lot of good it did to help this fellow. We protected his flocks in the wilderness, and nothing he owned was lost or stolen. But he has repaid me evil for good. May God strike me and kill me if even one man of his household is still alive tomorrow morning!
> When Abigail saw David, she quickly got off her

donkey and bowed low before him. She fell at his feet and said, "I accept all blame in this matter, my lord. Please listen to what I have to say. I know Nabal is a wicked and ill-tempered man; please don't pay any attention to him. He is a fool, just as his name suggests. But I never even saw the young men you sent …

"Here is a present that I, your servant, have brought to you and your young men. Please forgive me if I have offended you in any way. The LORD *will surely reward you with a lasting dynasty, for you are fighting the* LORD's *battles. And you have not done wrong throughout your entire life."*   —1 Samuel 25:20–28 (NLT)

Abigail stepped in to fix a wrong. She protected her household and kept David's anger from getting away from him. Because of Abigail's willingness to make a difference, many lives were saved.

Your Life

In your life, there may be a time when you need to provide help to someone. In our world there is much wrong that is being done. God is pleased when people reach out to others in care.

Our prayers and deeds can rescue others.

CHAPTER 21

JOHN HYDE

Praying When No One Is Looking

**When He Lived:
1865 – 1912 AD**

→ **1908 AD**

John Hyde prays for one soul a day

John Hyde sank onto his knees. The wooden floor was hard and made his legs ache, but his heart hurt even more.

The sky outside the small window was dark. Although his body was weary, John had no plans to sleep. His mind was focused on the lost souls—millions of them—in India. How could he sleep when there was such a great need?

As he bowed his head, John thought of his brother, Edmund. Edmund was the one who had his eyes set on being a missionary first, but with Edmund's sudden death, God placed the burden on John's heart. Even after all these years, John felt like a poor replacement for his brother.

Lord, I feel so inadequate for the task. It was a feeling

that John had a hard time shaking. Not only did he question his ability, but it seemed as if others questioned John's ability too.

When John was on the ship to India, he had received a letter from a close friend. "I will not cease praying for you until you be filled with the Holy Spirit," his friend had written.

Anger had surged through John as he'd read those words. Did this man think that the Holy Spirit did not dwell within him already?

The words played over and over in John's mind. Finally, he realized the man was right. On that ship—and every day afterward—John prayed for the same thing. If he was going to do any work in India, he needed the Spirit within him to do it.

When he arrived in India in 1892, John wanted to know God's Word more deeply. He had studied God's Word as much as he could. But John was partly deaf, and he had a hard time learning the native languages of India. John knew his own weaknesses, and he began to pray intensely. Starting in 1899, he began to spend entire nights in prayer.

John enjoyed his time in India. He had busy days and many people to talk to. The problem was that John never had enough time to pray. John knew that he needed prayer to connect him with God's Spirit. That's when John decided to pray in the quiet of the night. He'd given up sleep before, why shouldn't he now?

During his time in college, John had stayed up late to study. During holiday parties he'd also stayed up too, talking and laughing with friends. Surely he could manage giving up sleep for something far more important than studying books and partying. The souls of the Indians were much more important.

Outside the window, the birds' last songs had ended, but the noises of hyenas and jackals took their place. Mosquitoes and gnats buzzed around his head, mixing with croaks, rustles, and hums from the other night creatures. The sounds came from all directions, replacing the creak of carts from travelers, burden bearers, and bandy drivers. As he prayed, John knew that God was doing the work where he could not. He also knew that he needed to gather others to pray with him.

John created the Punjab Prayer Union. He asked the members to set aside half an hour a day to pray for spiritual revival in India. John knew that change would come only as they sank to their knees and sought for the souls of the men and women they desired to impact for Christ.

In 1908, John gathered with Indian Christians and western missionaries in Sialkot (in modern day Pakistan).

As they'd been doing in recent years, they gathered to pray for revival and spiritual renewal. This was their fourth year meeting together and praying. Many nights over the years, John stayed up praying, yet on this night a new urgency stirred in his chest. Warm heat seemed to flow through him, and a thought entered his mind that seemed both crazy and full of faith.

"Dear Lord, I know this is an impossible request, but I will ask it anyway." John took a deep breath and then released it. "Lord, during the coming year I pray that in India one soul would be saved every day."[114]

His lips moved slightly with the words, and he continued to plead for souls. John fixed his mind on the God of heaven. He knew that the battle would be fought at God's feet.

That year, 400 people committed themselves to Jesus through John's work. It was more than one a day. The next year when they gathered, John prayed a new prayer—for two souls a day. That year, indeed, 800 men and women became followers of Jesus Christ.

And in 1910, John Hyde found himself on his knees again. He and his fellow missionaries slept in a common room, and they'd fall asleep while John was still praying. His plea was fervent, "Give me souls, oh God, or I die!"

The meeting neared an end as John stood up in front of his co-laborers. "Friends, I'm praying for four souls a day, and nothing less."

In the coming year, John traveled through India. And he prayed as much as he taught. John soon became known as Praying Hyde.

Men from Calcutta, Bombay, and other large cities asked John to come to speak to them and to pray. During the day, Praying Hyde shared God's truth, and at night he prayed. Hyde would tell his friends that the burden for the souls of India was so great that he couldn't sleep until he felt that there was victory in the battle between good and evil that raged in the people around him. Daily, more men and women believed in Jesus, but the countless hours of working and praying began to take its toll on John.

One day after prayer, John's legs trembled as he stood. He held out his hand and allowed his friend to lead him. His health had deteriorated. In Calcutta, those who served with him began to worry.

"Friend, we must take you to see the doctor."

They sat and waited for the doctor's report and no one could have anticipated the answer. The burden on John Hyde's heart had affected him physically. His heart had shifted out of its natural position on the left side of his chest. It had moved to the right.[115]

"John, you have to get complete rest," the doctor told him, "or you won't live six months."

John Hyde returned home to the United States, but he did not stop praying. Praying from his family's home, John lived to learn that a revival had moved through the Punjab and the rest of India—a revival that changed history. A revival ignited by one man's prayers.

John's last words were: "Shout the victory of Jesus Christ!"

Today in India, millions of people have accepted Jesus Christ. Every moment John spent on his knees was multiplied for God's glory. John Hyde's humble prayers were answered in India, and history was forever changed.

We watch out for others by praying for them

When John got to India, he spent time in God's Word. He wanted to make sure that he knew the messages that God wanted him to share. Only after God's Word filled him from top to bottom did John start language lessons.

Reading God's Word helped John Hyde to know God's heart. He became a "watchman" for the people of India.

Isaiah 62:6 says, "I've posted watchmen on your walls, Jerusalem. Day and night they keep at it, praying, calling out, reminding GOD to remember. They are to give him no peace until he does what he said, until he makes Jerusalem famous as the City of Praise" (MSG). We can be watchmen for those who don't know God. Our prayers—day or night—will make a difference in their lives.

Something to Think About

A watchman will watch out for other people's needs. How can you be a watchman? How will God's Word prepare you for this task?

In His Own Words

The more John Hyde read God's Word and prayed, the more his heart was opened to the world. God loves all the world, and as we spend time with him in prayer, that love becomes ours too. This is what John said happened during one of his times in prayer:

> On the day of prayer, God gave me a new experience. I seemed to be away above our conflict here in the Punjab and I saw God's great battle in all India, and then away out beyond in China, Japan, and Africa. I saw how we had been thinking in narrow circles of our own countries and in our own denominations, and how God was now rapidly joining force to force and line to line, and all was beginning to be one great struggle. That, to me, means the great triumph of Christ. We must exercise the greatest care to be utterly obedient to Him who sees the battlefield all the time. It is only He who can put each man in the place where his life can count for the most.[116]

How He Changed History

During his time in India, John Hyde was only one of five missionaries in a territory with one million non-Christians. The people of India are in a caste system. This means that some groups of people have more privileges and opportunities than others. John Hyde preached that all men and women—no matter their position in the eyes of the world—had a place in God's kingdom. In a letter to his seminary he wrote: "Yesterday eight low-caste persons were baptized at one of the villages. It seems a work of God in which man, even as an instrument, was used in a very small degree."[117] John Hyde helped people in India look at themselves differently, and those who had very few opportunities in life received the greatest gift of all, salvation in Jesus Christ.

John Hyde earned the nickname "Praying Hyde" and his ministry led to revival. As a result, hundreds of pastors, teachers, and evangelists were called and trained to reach people. Thousands came to know Christ. Even after John's death, the movement continued, and by 1935 nearly half of the Chuhra caste had become Christians. The Christian faith also changed how people saw themselves. "During the 1920s and 1930s, many of these formerly Hindu Chuhras, now listed their caste as 'Christian,' migrated to other parts of India, including Sindh. At the time of partition the majority of the Christians in the new country of Pakistan traced their ancestry to grandparents or great-grandparents, converted to Christ out of the Chuhra caste."[118] What couldn't be changed outwardly through the government was changed inwardly by heart transformation.

it's in the Bible

Any time is a good time to pray, but it's important to find quiet times to pray, too. Jesus is an example of this.

Jesus was God. He could order angels to come to his aid. Jesus could command even the waves and the water to obey him, yet he still took time to be by himself and pray.

> As soon as the meal was finished, Jesus insisted that the disciples get in the boat and go on ahead across to Bethsaida while he dismissed the congregation. After sending them off, he climbed a mountain to pray.
>
> Late at night, the boat was far out at sea; Jesus was still by himself on land. He could see his men struggling with the oars, the wind having come up against them. At about four o'clock in the morning, Jesus came toward them, walking on the sea.   —Mark 6:46–48 (MSG)

The multitudes pressed around Jesus during the day. They wanted to hear about God's coming kingdom. The people had needs, and Jesus met them. And Jesus' night hours were for prayer.

John Hyde followed Jesus' example. He prayed into, and through, the night.

Sometimes we feel we need to *do* more, but really we need to *pray* more. Like John Hyde learned, prayer allows God to do the work we cannot do on our own.

Your Life

Do you have a quiet time set aside to read your Bible and pray? There are many important things we can do, but nothing is more important than spending time with God in prayer. Think about your day. When would be a good time to find a quiet place to pray? Where would that place be?

Once you think of a time and place, then make an effort to spend time with God. You'll never know how it can change your life and the lives of others!

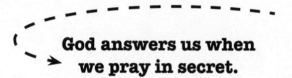

God answers us when we pray in secret.

CHAPTER 22

MOTHER TERESA

Prayers for the Poor and Forgotten

Eddie Adams/AP Images

When She Lived: 1910 – 1997 AD

⟶ 1922 AD

One girl's humble prayer leads millions to the love of God

Anjezëe (Agnes) Gonxhe Bojaxhiu grew up fascinated by the lives of missionaries. Her father died when she was young, but her mother went to work and the family was well cared for. Her mother was also a strong pillar of faith for her young daughter. Whenever Agnes needed help, her mother would speak to her with gentleness, saying, "Child, put your hand in the hand of Jesus. Walk all the way with him."

As a young girl, Agnes walked the cobblestone streets of Skopje in southern Yugoslavia. It was a mostly Muslim city, but Agnes knew the true God, and she attended Catholic mass daily, knowing there was no place she'd rather be. One Wednesday evening, she joined a group of preteen girls as they listened to a letter being read. It was from a local priest who'd left for the mission field in India. Tears filled Agnes's eyes.

Agnes heard about the poverty and suffering of those in India. She listened as the letter told about the cruel caste system. The caste system meant that from birth there were those who would grow up only being allowed to work with garbage and human waste. They could never get a better job, just because they were born into a certain family.

After the letter was read, Agnes turned to her friend, "Mary, wouldn't it be wonderful to be a missionary? I want to help people and bring them God's love." At thirteen years old, Agnes knew she wanted to commit herself to God's service in India, but her friends didn't understand. Why wouldn't she stay in Skopje—where so many were in need of the same thing?

When the meeting was over, Agnes slipped into the church to pray alone. "Lord, show me the way." Her plea came from deep in her heart. She thought about her mother's words, and she rose from the hard floor. Agnes held up her hand, as if reaching for Jesus. She imagined him taking her hand. She also trusted that he'd show her the way.

Six years passed, and finally the time had come. In 1928, the same missionary priest returned to Skopje. He told her the Missionary Sisters of Loretto were looking for young women to teach in their schools. They needed help in India. Agnes knew this was Jesus' answer to her prayer. This was Jesus' leading. Agnes left home at the age of 18 to join the Sisters of Loretto as a missionary.

"Agnes," her mother told her as she left, "this is what you have prayed for all these years. If Jesus is calling you to this work, then everything will turn out all right." Agnes left, but she never saw her mother or sister again.

Agnes took her solemn vows as a Catholic nun on May 14, 1937. She chose to be named after Saint Thérèse de Lisiequx, choosing the Spanish spelling, Teresa.[119] Sister Teresa started by teaching school in Calcutta, but her mind and heart continually turned to the poverty surrounding her in Calcutta.

Then one day, on a train to Darjeeling, she received her second call. For the rest of her life, she referred to it as "the call within the call." As Sister Teresa thought again of the poorest of the poor, she had a feeling deep down that she was supposed to serve them.

Lord, make it clear to me what you ask, she prayed. And as she rode along, she knew she was, "to quench the infinite thirst of Jesus on the cross for love and souls" by "laboring at the salvation and sanctification of the poorest of the poor."[120]

Something stirring inside her told Sister Teresa that God was asking her to leave the convent and work with the poor. She was to live among them. Two years later, in 1948, the Vatican granted her permission to leave the Sisters of Loretto. Teresa started working with the children of the poor in the slums. She also learned basic medicine and went into the homes of the sick to care for them. As her students grew older, some of them joined her. Yet still there were so many more who needed help.

Sister Teresa—called Mother Teresa by the children—walked the streets, and her heart ached. Men, women, and children who were close to death were abandoned there—discarded and alone. Turned away by local hospitals, they had nowhere to go. Mother Teresa, and those who helped her, rented a room. A year later, they were established by the church, and they were soon known as the Missionaries of Charity.

The Missionaries of Charity's work expanded within Calcutta and throughout India. Then it grew, moving to Venezuela, Africa, Australia, the Middle East, and North America.

People all over the world started paying attention to Mother Teresa's work, and a documentary film called *Something Beautiful for God* (1969) drew lots of attention. Mother Teresa's heart pounded every time someone wanted to interview her about her work, but she realized her job was not only to care for those in need, but also to encourage others to do the same.

In 1979, Mother Teresa was awarded the Nobel Peace Prize, and in 1985 she opened "Gift of Love" in New York, her first house for AIDS patients. Mother Teresa continued to serve until just months before she passed away. When she died, over 4,000 sisters operated 610 missions in 123 countries, caring for the poorest of the poor.[121]

Jesus had indeed answered Mother Teresa's prayers and led her by the hand, and millions were impacted as a result. Mother Teresa never set out to be an icon of faith, but because of her, Jesus became known to many. Her journey all started with the prayer of a young girl, and history was forever changed.

You gain so much when you give your life away

Agnes could have lived a normal life in the city of Skopje. It could have been a good life of caring for others and of service. And if she'd chosen for herself, maybe that's what she would have picked. Instead, Agnes let God choose, and she became Mother Teresa. She humbled herself in prayer. She lifted her hand up to God and let him lead her, and he led her all over the world with a message of Christian love and charity.

Agnes gave up her life, just as Jesus gave up his for her … and for all of us. Ephesians 5:1–2 says: "Follow God's example, therefore, as dearly loved children and walk in the way of love, just as Christ loved us and gave himself up for us as a fragrant offering and sacrifice to God."

If we let him, God can do much more with our lives than we'd ever imagine possible.

Something to Think About

What plans do you have for your life? Do you think God's plans for you are different or the same as your plans? Take a few minutes and pray to God. Lift your hand to him and ask him to lead you. How do you feel knowing you are in God's hands and that he has a good plan for you?

In Her Own Words

Mother Teresa prayed this daily:

> DEAR JESUS, help me to spread Thy fragrance everywhere I go. Flood my soul with Thy spirit and love. Penetrate and possess my whole being so utterly that all my life may only be a radiance of Thine. Shine through me and be so in me that every soul I come in contact with may feel Thy presence in my soul. Let them look up and see no longer me but only Jesus. Stay with me and then I shall begin to shine as you shine, so to shine as to be a light to others.[122]

How She Changed History

Mother Teresa founded the Missionaries of Charity, branches of which are active in 133 countries. These missions help the poor and desperate all over the world. It is Mother Teresa's excellent example that inspires others to give to those in need.

Mother Teresa is so well known for how she impacted lives, that every year since 2005, awards have been given to honor individuals and organizations that promote peace, equality, and social justice. The award is given in her honor and is called the Mother Teresa Award.

it's in the Bible

God has shown us through the Bible, and throughout history, that age does not matter when it comes to choosing someone to do great things for him. This was the case for a small boy in First Samuel:

> *Meanwhile, the boy Samuel served the LORD by assisting Eli. Now in those days messages from the LORD were very rare, and visions were quite uncommon.*
>
> *One night Eli, who was almost blind by now, had gone to bed. The lamp of God had not yet gone out, and Samuel was sleeping in the Tabernacle near the Ark of God. Suddenly the LORD called out, "Samuel!"*
>
> *"Yes?" Samuel replied. "What is it?" He got up and ran to Eli. "Here I am. Did you call me?"*
>
> *"I didn't call you," Eli replied. "Go back to bed." So he did.*
>
> *Then the LORD called out again, "Samuel!"*
>
> *Again Samuel got up and went to Eli. "Here I am. Did you call me?"*
>
> *"I didn't call you, my son," Eli said. "Go back to bed."*
>
> *Samuel did not yet know the LORD because he had never had a message from the LORD before. So the LORD called a third time, and once more Samuel got up and went to Eli. "Here I am. Did you call me?"*
>
> *Then Eli realized it was the LORD who was calling the boy. So he said to Samuel, "Go and lie down again, and if someone calls again, say, 'Speak, LORD, your servant is listening.'" So Samuel went back to bed.*
>
> *And the LORD came and called as before, "Samuel! Samuel!"*
>
> *And Samuel replied, "Speak, your servant is listening."*
>
> *—1 Samuel 3:1–10 (NLT)*

As a young boy, Samuel was called by God to be a priest and a leader in Israel. God speaks to men, women, and children too. If you seek him and listen, God will speak to you—not in a voice you can hear with your ears, but in a stirring deep in your heart. God will give you a burden for a person or group of people who need compassion and love, and it will be up to you to love them as Jesus would.

Your Life

Agnes dared to seek God and offer her life to him at a young age. She grew to become Mother Teresa, one of the most well-known and cherished women in history. And what God did with Mother Teresa, he can do with you. Like Mother Teresa, pray daily that you will be the fragrance of Jesus wherever you go. Pray that others will see Jesus as you serve them.

When you give yourself to God, your life—and the lives of others—will forever be changed.

CHAPTER 23

THE BRITISH PEOPLE OF WWII

King and Country Pray Together

Walter Bellamy/Stringer/Getty Images

When They Lived: 1939 – 1945 AD

⟶ 1940 AD

A nation prays and a country is saved

The nation of Great Britain was in trouble. In 1933, a man named Adolf Hitler became ruler of Germany. He was set on making all of Europe his. In September 1939, Hitler and his army, called the Nazis, invaded Poland. Very quickly the Nazis also took over Norway, Denmark, Holland, Luxembourg, and Belgium without much resistance. Hitler turned to France after that. The French did their best to hold their ground, but they gave up after forty days.

The English people were certain that Hitler would try to take control of their country next. But Winston Churchill, the prime minister, wasn't about to submit so easily. "We would rather go down fighting than be enslaved to Germany," he said. They were also worried about their troops on French soil. Hitler was advancing quickly, and if he continued, their troops would soon be captured or killed.

The country needed prayer. Badly. But would they submit to God? Would they turn over their need to him?

At first, in April 1940, the Archbishop of Canterbury didn't want to set aside a special day of prayer. He was afraid it would be "misunderstood or rather misrepresented by the enemy."[123] After all, if they were praying, that would prove they were almost defeated, right?

Soon things got so bad that it didn't matter what the Germans thought. The British Empire needed prayer ... now. On May 23, King George VI proclaimed a Day of National Prayer to be held on Sunday, May 26, throughout the Empire. Little did he know that his request would come at the exact moment it was needed. On May 24, just a day after the Archbishop had chosen a day of prayer, 500,000 British and French soldiers were trapped on the beach of Dunkirk when the Germans took control of France. Fear gripped the heart of the British people. If the Nazis advanced, it would be easy to wipe out all those men. Husbands, sons, and brothers would be killed. They faced certain annihilation.

Two days later, on May 26, the British people gathered to pray. They pleaded with God to save the soldiers they loved. The British Broadcasting Corporation (BBC) broadcasted three services. The king and members of the Cabinet attended the services at Westminster Abbey. Outside, the church was surrounded by large groups of people who couldn't get in. Millions of the king's subjects, in England and all over the world, joined together in churches to pray.

Instead of moving in, the Nazis retreated. Hitler stopped the advance of his armored columns right at the point that they could have completely destroyed the Allied forces. Hitler's own generals didn't understand this decision. This was the first miracle.

Hitler held back, but British leaders didn't know for how long. England made the decision to evacuate the troops from France, but there was a problem. The only port they could evacuate from was Dunkirk. And that port was being threatened by the Germans. Best estimates were that they'd be able to evacuate only 20,000 or 30,000 men, perhaps half of the people there.

Then the second miracle occurred on May 28. Storms broke out over Flanders, in Belgium, grounding the German Luftwaffe (air force). They could not bomb any of the Allied troops. This allowed the British army to journey 12 miles to Dunkirk on foot. They walked in the darkness of the storm, but they were safe from bombing and attacks.

Then, the third miracle arrived. For six days following the National Day of Prayer, the normally rough waters of the English Channel were calm. Even though the storm raged so the planes couldn't fly, the waters remained still.

Small boats and yachts, warships, and privately owned

cruisers were sent to retrieve the men. The channel was so filled it looked like rush hour traffic on a highway. On May 29, 47,000 men were rescued. On May 30, 53,000. On May 31, 68,000. On June 1, 64,000. In total, 334,000 men found their way to safety. British Field Marshal William Edmund Ironside later wrote, "I still cannot understand how it is that the [Germans] have allowed us to get [our troops] off in this way. It is almost fantastic that we have been able to do it in the face of all the bombing and gunning."[124]

His troops remained in place until early June. God held back Hitler's hand until all the troops could be safely evacuated.

The hand of God was seen so clearly, that Sunday, June 9, was appointed as a Day of National Thanksgiving, and history was forever changed.

All God asks is that we turn to him

In this life we will face many troubles, but we do not have to face them alone. No matter how far we've gone away from God, we can always turn back to him. When we do, he is ready to assist us in amazing ways. When is the right time to pray? Now!

That is why the Lord says:

> *Turn to me now, while there is time.*
> *Give me your hearts.*
> *Come with fasting, weeping, and mourning.*
> *Don't tear your clothing in your grief,*
> *but tear your hearts instead."*
> *Return to the LORD your God,*
> *for he is merciful and compassionate,*

slow to get angry and filled with unfailing love.
   He is eager to relent and not punish.
Who knows? Perhaps he will give you a reprieve,
   sending you a blessing instead of this curse.
Perhaps you will be able to offer grain and wine
   to the LORD your God as before.

                             —*Joel 2:12 – 14 (NLT)*

Something to Think About

Why do we often wait before praying? What did the British people discover when they gathered together to pray? What do you need to pray about? Whom can you get to join you?

In Their Own Words

On May 26, 1940, the former prime minister of Great Britain, Neville Chamberlain, wrote: "May 26th, Blackest day of all … this was the National Day of Prayer?"

Even as they prayed, it seemed as if all would be lost.

And on May 27, the German High Command went so far as to boast, "The British army is encircled and our troops are proceeding to its annihilation."

Even as the German High Command boasted, they did not take God into account.

What Mr. Chamberlain and the German High Command couldn't see was that God had good plans to protect the soldiers. The evacuation of Dunkirk turned out to be one of the most dramatic turning points of the war.

What appeared to be a defeat became a series of miracles because of God's saving grace.

How They Changed History

The British people were weary from war, yet as their worries increased, they believed they only had one hope—they must turn to God. The people came together in prayer, and when Hitler did not invade, their confidence grew. Maybe they could make it through the war after all. Maybe Hitler *could* be defeated.

Because the British and French soldiers were evacuated instead of captured, they were able to stand up to the Germans and Italians in North Africa the following year. Hitler's decision not to invade is considered one of the top ten military blunders of World War II.[125] Yet, what historians consider a mistake, the British people consider a miracle.

The Nazis turned their attention to Russia instead of Great Britain, and eventually Hitler was defeated there. Knowing that his army would have to surrender, Hitler took his own life on April 20, 1945 and Germany surrendered on May 7, 1945.

it's in the Bible

In the Old Testament, the Jews in exile faced a serious problem, and they also used prayer to help their nation. They lived under the rule of a foreign king, and one of the high officials wanted to cause trouble. A law was made that all Jews must be killed, but the king had no idea that his wife, Esther, was a Jew.

Esther was troubled. She didn't want to see her people wiped out. But if Esther went before the king without being called for, she would be killed. Esther asked all the Jews to fast and pray for three days. Her kinsman Mordecai wrote this to her:

> *"Don't think for a moment that because you're in the palace you will escape when all other Jews are killed. If you keep quiet at a time like this, deliverance and relief for the Jews will arise from some other place, but you and your relatives will die. Who knows if perhaps you were made queen for just such a time as this?"*
>
> *Then Esther sent this reply to Mordecai: "Go and gather together all the Jews of Susa and fast for me. Do not eat or drink for three days, night or day. My maids and I will do the same. And then, though it is against the law, I will go in to see the king. If I must die, I must die." So Mordecai went away and did everything as Esther had ordered him.*   —*Esther 4:13–17 (NLT)*

Esther was willing to risk her life, but she asked the people for one thing—to pray. The people did, and their prayers were answered. God turned the king's heart so he'd not only protect the people, but that they'd also be blessed.

> *Then Mordecai left the king's presence, wearing the royal robe of blue and white, the great crown of gold, and an outer cloak of fine linen and purple. And the people of Susa celebrated the new decree. The Jews were filled with joy and gladness and were honored everywhere. In every province and city, wherever the king's decree arrived, the Jews rejoiced and had a great celebration and declared a public festival and holiday. And many of the people of the land became Jews themselves, for they feared what the Jews might do to them.*   —*Esther 8:15–17 (NLT)*

Your Life

Have you thought about praying for your nation? Have you thought about getting others to join together and pray with you? It is so much easier to complain than it is to pray. It's easy to see all the problems in our country, but not do anything about it.

When we pray, we take our eyes off the problem and put our eyes on God. We are reminded that he holds the whole world in his hands. He can defeat even the biggest threat we have with ease.

The next time that you start to worry about all the problems in our country and in the world, get on your knees to pray. Better yet, ask people to join you.

Nations that pray together can see miracles happen.

CORRIE TEN BOOM

Prayers for an Enemy

When She Lived: 1892–1983 AD

➤ 1944 AD

Corrie's prayers carried her through Nazi torment

Corrie ten Boom staggered through the concrete wash room. Her clothes and shoes had been taken away, and prison guards shouted angrily at some women and beat others. Corrie and her sister Betsie stood among the other fearful women. Corrie had lived an ordinary life as a watchmaker before the start of the Second World War, but now she was a criminal—at least in the eyes of the Nazi Germans. *Dear God, please do not leave us. Please be with us*, she prayed.

Prayer came naturally to Corrie. Her parents made prayer an important part of her life. Her parents taught her to pray, and they lived an example of prayer. Corrie's grandfather, Willem ten Boom, felt the need to pray for Jewish people after a moving worship service. In 1844, the ten Boom family, along with friends and neighbors, started a weekly prayer meeting for Jewish people. Every week they specifically prayed for the peace of Jerusalem as talked about in Psalm 122:6. "Pray for the peace of Jerusalem: they shall prosper that love thee" (KJV). These meetings took place every week for one hundred years. They stopped on February 28, 1944, when Nazi soldiers came to the house to take the family away.[126]

Corrie's family also worked to hide Jews in their home during the Nazi occupation of Holland. The Germans had been sending the Jews to death camps, and Corrie and her family couldn't stand by and watch without trying to help. For many years they helped by hiding men, women, and children behind a secret wall in their house, but eventually they were caught. Corrie's whole family was arrested in February of 1944.

Corrie's father died ten days after his arrest. Corrie and her sister Betsie were transferred to the Ravensbrück concentration camp, near Berlin. But when almost everything she owned had been taken away, Corrie managed to keep a secret Bible. And when Corrie had nothing else, she had God's Word and prayer.

The women in the barracks with Corrie and Betsie had faced great pain. Some had been beaten. Others had lost family members. They'd been taken from their homes and locked up as criminals. Corrie knew they needed to hear about God's love. Even though her actions could get her in trouble, in the evenings, Corrie gathered the women to read God's Word and pray. Because Corrie was willing to risk her life to bring the Good News of Jesus to others, the crowded, filthy Barracks 28 became a prayer room.

Corrie and Betsie had first been nervous to gather the women around for Bible reading and prayer, but when they discovered that no guards bothered them (because of the lice spreading through the barracks) they grew bolder. As they gathered, some women whispered hymns while others recited meaningful prayers. Then Corrie or Betsie would open the Bible, translating the Dutch to German. God's Word continued to be translated down the aisles in French, Polish, Russian, Czech, and back into Dutch.[127]

Betsie had struggled with sickness her whole life, and her body couldn't take the starvation and abuses of the concentration camp for long. Betsie died on December 16, 1944, leaving Corrie to face the horrors of the camp alone. Until the end, Betsie's desire was that others know the love of God. "(We) must tell them what we have learned here. We must tell them that there is no pit so deep that he is not deeper still," Betsie once said. "They will listen to us, Corrie, because we have been there."[128] These were some of the last words Betsie ever spoke to Corrie.

Due to a clerical error, Corrie was released from Ravensbrück one week before all the women her age were killed. This is how Corrie described it later.

" 'Follow me,' a young girl in an officer's uniform said to me. I walked slowly through the gate, never looking back. Behind me I heard the hinges squeak as the gate swung shut. I was free and flooding through my mind were the words of Jesus to the church at Philadelphia: 'Behold,

I have set before thee an open door, and no man can shut it ...' (Revelation 3:8)."[129]

She returned to her home in Haarlem and went back to her work as a watchmaker, but soon discovered that her former life no longer satisfied her. Instead she traveled and told her family's story and the lessons she'd learned in the concentration camp. When the war was over, Corrie helped to open a home for former camp inmates.

Because of the sacrifice of the ten Boom family, over 800 Jews were saved from Nazi death camps. Many women in Ravensbrück became Christians because of Corrie and Betsie's witness to them. Until her death on her ninety-first birthday, Corrie continued to tell anyone who'd listen what she had learned. She traveled to more than sixty countries, sharing the good news of sacrifice, prayer, and forgiveness, and history was forever changed.

Sometimes the hardest trial we face is forgiving our enemy

Corrie faced hardship in the war, but one of the hardest trials came two years after the war ended. In 1947, Corrie was teaching in Munich, Germany. Germany had just been defeated in World War II, and Corrie had come to the country to share the message of God's forgiveness.

Through the crowd, a man approached her. Even though he wore a brown overcoat and hat, she perfectly pictured the blue uniform and the cap with the skull and crossbones of a Nazi SS guard. She knew him. He'd been one of the guards at Ravensbrück.

Pain shot through her chest. Anger and fear filled her mind, and her whole body trembled at seeing him. He'd been one of the cruelest guards. She had spoken to many, telling them of God's forgiveness, but now—looking at her enemy—she had only hatred for this man in her heart.

"You mentioned Ravensbrück in your talk," the man said. "I was a guard there, but since that time I became a Christian. I know that God has forgiven me for the cruel things I did there, but I would like to hear it from your lips as well. Fräulein ... will you forgive me?" He extended his hand to her.[130]

With his words, a thousand thoughts went through Corrie's mind. She remembered how her sister Betsie died in horrible conditions, how so many women had suffered in the camp. Corrie looked at the man's hand and struggled to extend her hand to him. This was one of the most difficult things she'd ever faced.

Yet Corrie knew she had to do it. She had to forgive. She thought of Matthew 6:15, "But if you do not forgive others their sins, your Father will not forgive your sins." Corrie knew that forgiveness wasn't a feeling. She had to will herself to forgive.

"Jesus, help me!" she prayed silently. "I can lift my hand. I can do that much. You supply the feeling."

Corrie extended her hand to the man before her, and as she did, a miracle happened. A current started in her shoulder, raced down her arm, and sprang into their joined hands. Warmth flooded her whole being.

Tears filled her eyes, "I forgive you, brother. With all my heart." God's love flowed through Corrie as it never had before,[131] showing that forgiveness is possible even for those who've created great offenses against us. Through Corrie's story, people from all over the world have come to understand the Holocaust better, yet they've also come to understand God's mercy better, too. And history was forever changed.

Something to Think About ⌐⌐⌐⌐⌐⌐⌐⌐⌐⌐⌐⌐⌐⌐⌐➤

When is a time that you had to forgive someone who hurt you? Was forgiving that person hard or easy? How can God help you when you want to forgive? What words can you pray when you feel that you are unable to forgive?

In Her Own Words

Corrie traveled the world, sharing the power of forgiveness. She wrote these words in one of her notebooks. Later these words were published in a book.

"Forgiveness is the key that unlocks the door of resentment and the handcuffs of hatred. It is a power that breaks the chains of bitterness and the shackles of selfishness."[132]

How She Changed History

Along with her family, Corrie ten Boom helped many Jews escaping certain death at the hands of the Nazis, including six people hiding in their home when the family was arrested. During her imprisonment, Corrie provided comfort to those jailed with her. And, after the war, she returned to the Netherlands and set up a rehabilitation center for concentration camp survivors. She even set up a shelter for the Dutch people who previously worked with the Germans, and it was a visible sign of loving her enemies.

For 40 years, Corrie traveled the world speaking in churches and conferences. She also went to secret Bible study groups in countries where Christians were persecuted for believing in Christ. "Because she had suffered, too, she could tell them that God is fully able to shine His light anywhere."[133] After hearing Corrie's story, many people have learned how to forgive and have gone on to live more peaceful lives.

it's in the Bible

The Bible speaks often about forgiveness and about loving our enemies. There is no greater example of this than Jesus' pleas for forgiveness for his enemies on the cross:

> And when they came to the place that is called The Skull, there they crucified him, and the criminals, one on his right and one on his left. And Jesus said, "Father, forgive them, for they know not what they do." And they cast lots to divide his garments ... Then Jesus, calling out with a loud voice, said, "Father, into your hands I commit my spirit!" And having said this he breathed his last.
>
> —Luke 23:33–34, 46 (ESV)

Jesus is the reason we can be forgiven, and he is the reason we can forgive others. Forgiving others does not mean accepting what they have done. It's not ignoring our hurt. Forgiving others is an extension of what God has done in our lives by forgiving us.

Prayer can help prepare us to forgive others. On the

night before he was crucified, Jesus went to the mountain to pray. Prayer strengthens us for what we face and allows God to work through us when we're willing to seek him for strength.

Your Life

Corrie's family faced horrible pain and loss, yet they stood firm in their faith. They stayed strong because of prayer. For 100 years her family had been praying for the Jewish people, and those prayers prepared them for what was to come. Prayer allowed Corrie's family to be strong when they were needed to protect others. Prayer also helped Corrie to forgive and to push away the pain and anger in her heart.

Prayer allows you to be strong and to forgive.

CHAPTER 25

DIETRICH BONHOEFFER

Prayers for the Future

© SZ Photo/Scherl/Bridgeman Images

When He Lived: 1906 – 1945 AD

→ **1945 AD**

Dietrich Bonhoeffer gives his life for his faith

There are many people who are remembered for the type of life they lived, but Dietrich Bonhoeffer is also known for his death. Near the end of World War II, the Allied forces had already made their way into Germany. Many hoped that victory against the Nazis would come soon. But Dietrich knew that if the Allied forced defeated the ungodly Nazis, he wouldn't live to see it. He was condemned to die.

On Monday, April 9, 1945, Dietrich knelt on the floor in prayer. He believed in Jesus, and he knew that heaven awaited him. He had continued to do what was right—even in the midst of war—and now his fight was done. He heard the guards' booted footsteps nearing and knew the men were coming to take him away. Dietrich whispered one more prayer of strength, and then he rose.

The morning air was crisp as Dietrich walked to his death. Little did he know that one German doctor watched him.

> I saw Pastor Bonhoeffer ... kneeling on the floor praying fervently to God. I was most deeply moved by the way this lovable man prayed, so devout and so certain that God heard his prayer. At the place of execution, he again said a short prayer and then climbed the few steps to the gallows, brave and composed. His death ensued after a few seconds. In the almost fifty years that I worked as a doctor, I have hardly ever seen a man die so entirely submissive to the will of God.[134]

Dietrich left the world that had been filled with murder, fighting, and loss for the last ten years, and entered the presence of God.

Perhaps Dietrich had expected this day for a while.

From the moment Adolf Hitler came into power in 1933, Dietrich had been troubled. He was a Protestant pastor, and right before his eyes Hitler was leading the people away from God toward a new regime of cruelty where Hitler was the final authority.

Seeing the dangers of Nazism, Dietrich joined with other pastors to form the Confessing Church. Their goal was to remind the people of God's true Word, so they would not be swayed by Nazi beliefs.

Dietrich was a passionate writer and speaker, and he helped people understand Jesus better. He helped people understand that they could be faithful followers of Jesus even with all the evil happening around them. "Jesus Christ lived in the midst of his enemies. At the end all his disciples deserted him. On the Cross he was utterly alone, surrounded by evildoers and mockers. For this cause he had come, to bring peace to the enemies of God ... The kingdom is to be in the midst of your enemies. And he who will not suffer this does not want to be of the Kingdom of Christ."[135]

But Dietrich's road was not easy. At one point, he felt that he wasn't making a difference in Germany and went to the United States for a time. But while he was there, his heart was still with his country, and he felt compelled to return.

Dietrich knew that most teens in Germany knew right from wrong, but they were impressionable. It was easy for them to be caught up in this new, exciting movement that seemingly held so much promise. They didn't fully understand the evil of the Nazi regime. Worried they would be swayed by Hitler's unholy promises, Dietrich accepted a position at a seminary — a school for young men who wanted to become pastors. He gave Bible talks, but he also spoke out against the evil happening in their nation. He knew Hitler was killing the weak, the disabled, and the elderly. Hitler was also persecuting the Jewish people.

While Dietrich's students were paying attention, the Gestapo (German police) was too. Dietrich was arrested and put in prison. He was condemned by the Nazis for his involvement in "Operation 7," a rescue mission that helped a small group of Jews escape over the German border and into Switzerland.[136] But even in prison Dietrich reached out to the other inmates to share Christ's love.

Later, Dietrich was sent to a Nazi concentration camp. He was put on trial for supposedly being involved in a plot to kill Hitler. His punishment was to hang on the gallows.

As he awaited his death, Dietrich prayed that the Nazi regime would be defeated. Four weeks later, the Allied forces were victorious.

Although Dietrich didn't live to see that victory, his prayers were answered in a mighty way. The man who wanted to influence younger generations still speaks through his books. His faith continues to inspire believers to stand up for what is right and true, and history is forever changed.

Our story doesn't end in our death

Even though Dietrich was in a prison cell, God was with him, building him up. Dietrich stood strong until the end because God was on his side. As he walked to the gallows, Dietrich's mind was no longer focused on what was seen, but what was unseen. "Therefore we do not lose heart. Though outwardly we are wasting away, yet inwardly we are being renewed day by day. For our light and momentary troubles are achieving for us an eternal glory that far outweighs them all. So we fix our eyes not on what is seen, but on what is unseen, since what is seen is temporary, but what is unseen is eternal." (2 Corinthians 4:16–17).

In life, there are times when we will be our weakest. But when we look to God's glory ahead, we understand that what we face on earth can't compare to whom we'll face in heaven.

Something to Think About

Why doesn't God always answer our prayers in a way that seems fair? How does hardship prepare us for heaven? When is a time that you faced a hard situation yet found God there?

In His Own Words

In a letter smuggled out of prison, Dietrich showed no bitterness toward his enemies. Instead, he saw how God was working all things for good.

> We in the resistance have learned to see the great events of world history from below; from the perspective of the excluded, the ill-treated, the powerless, the oppressed and despised ... so that personal suffering has become a more useful key for understanding the world than personal happiness.[137]

How He Changed History

Dietrich Bonhoeffer's theology and his work as a pastor have inspired many throughout the world and in various denominations. He united a community of believers during a time of hardship through the Preachers' Seminary. Unlike many other German pastors of the day, Bonhoeffer spoke out about the wrongness of the Nazi dictatorship and their treatment of Jews and other minorities. He was an active member of a secret group trying to undermine the Nazi government.

Dietrich Bonhoeffer's books have been read by tens of thousands of Christians, and they continue to encourage and inspire people today. Dietrich was convinced that it was impossible to be a follower of Jesus Christ apart from being connected with local believers: "Christianity means community through Jesus Christ and in Jesus Christ."[138]

Dietrich Bonhoeffer influenced Martin Luther King, Jr. and the Civil Rights Movement in the United States. His words also helped those who were fighting against communism in Eastern Europe during the Cold War and the anti-Apartheid movement in South Africa (which worked to bring equality between whites and non-whites).[139] Dietrich is known as someone who lived what he believed. His martyrdom (which means dying for what he believed) has been a great inspiration for Christians from all denominations.

it's in the Bible

In God's Word, we learn to trust the future. One of the forefathers of the nation of Israel also did this. Joseph was old, and his people were foreigners in Egypt. Joseph knew he would be buried in Egypt, but he believed that someday—even when he wasn't around—God would lead the Israelites back to the Promised Land. Joseph made the sons of Israel promise that when they left someday, they would take his bones with them.

> *"Soon I will die," Joseph told his brothers, "but God will surely come to help you and lead you out of this land of Egypt. He will bring you back to the land he solemnly promised to give to Abraham, to Isaac, and to Jacob."*
>
> *Then Joseph made the sons of Israel swear an oath,*

*and he said, "When God comes to help you and lead you
back, you must take my bones with you."*

—*Genesis 50:24–25 (NLT)*

Joseph didn't say, "If God comes to help you." Joseph
said, "When God comes to help you." Like Dietrich, Joseph
knew of God's faithfulness. He trusted God until the end.

Your Life

Everyone on earth only has a certain number of days,
but the amazing thing is that our prayers live on! Joseph's
prayer was answered 400 years after his death! Dietrich's
prayer that the Nazis would be defeated was answered in
less than a month.

Our stories don't end when our time on earth is done.
Dietrich's story is told over and over again every time
someone picks up one of his books. Our prayers don't end
during our time on earth either. God answers our prayers
according to his timing, not ours.

You, too, only have a certain number of days, but the
prayers you pray can be answered long after you are gone.
Your prayers matter, not just for today or for tomorrow.
Your prayers matter through your lifetime and beyond.

**There are times we might not see
the answers to our prayers —
but God is still faithful.**

NOTES

1. Herzel, Catherine, *Great Christians: Their Response and Witness* (Philadelphia: Lutheran Church Press, 1964), 10.
2. "Polycarp, Bishop of Smyrna and Martyr." *Polycarp, Bishop of Smyrna and Martyr.* N.p., n.d. Web. 07 Nov. 2014. <http://justus.anglican.org/resources/bio/108.html>.
3. "St. Polycarp: Saint of the Day: AmericanCatholic.org." *St. Polycarp, Saint of the Day, AmericanCatholic.org.* N.p., n.d. Web. 07 Nov. 2014. <http://www.americancatholic.org/Features/Saints/saint.aspx?id=1300>.
4. Wayne A. Meeks, et al., "The Martyrs," *Frontline: From Jesus to Christ.* Apr. 1998. Web 27 Nov. 2015. <http://www,pbs.org/wgbh/pages/frontline/shows/religion/why/martyrs.html>.
5. "Battle of the Milvian Bridge." *Wikipedia.* Wikimedia Foundation, 11 Mar. 2014. Web. 07 Nov. 2014. <http://en.wikipedia.org/wiki/Battle_of_the_Milvian_Bridge>.
6. John M. Mulder and Hugh Thomas, eds., *Finding God: A Treasury of Conversion Stories* (Grand Rapids, MI: Wm. Be. Eerdmans Publishing, 2012), 12.
7. Ibid., 8.

8. "Battle of the Milvian Bridge."

9. "Church History (Book IX)." *CHURCH FATHERS: Church History, Book IX (Eusebius)*. N.p., n.d. Web. 07 Nov. 2014. <http://www.newadvent.org/ fathers/250109.htm>.

10. "Constantine the Great." *CATHOLIC ENCYCLOPEDIA*. N.p., n.d. Web. 07 Nov. 2014. <http://www.newadvent.org/cathen/04295c.htm>.

11. Pamphilus, Eusebius, *The Life of the Blessed Emperor Constantine: From AD 306 to AD 337* (Arx Pub, 2009), 172.

12. Davis, Paul K., *100 Decisive Battles from Ancient Times to the Present: The World's Major Battles and How They Shaped History* (Oxford: Oxford University Press, 1999), 78.

13. "St. Patrick - Saints & Angels - Catholic Online." *St. Patrick - Saints & Angels - Catholic Online*. N.p., n.d. Web. 06 Nov. 2014. <http://www.catholic.org/saints/ saint.php?saint_id=89>.

14. "The Life of Saint Patrick." *FaithTalk 970*. N.p., n.d. Web. 07 Nov. 2014. <http://www.faithtalk970.com/ parenting/1129354/>.

15. "Contact Support." *Contact Support*. N.p., n.d. Web. 07 Nov. 2014. <http://celticchristianity.org/library/ patrick.html>.

16. "The Life of Saint Patrick."

17. "Confession of St. Patrick." *Christian Classics Ethereal Library*. N.p., n.d. Web. 06 Nov. 2014. <http://www.ccel.org/ccel/patrick/confession/ confession.html>, 37.

18. "St. Patrick - Saints & Angels - Catholic Online."

19. "The Life of Saint Patrick." *TrueTalk 800.* N.p., n.d. Web. 07 Nov. 2014. <http://www.truetalk800 .com/1129354/page2/>.

20. "Oswald a Battle Martyr." *Christianity.com.* N.p., n.d. Web. 07 Nov. 2014. <http://www.christianity. com/church/church-history/timeline/601-900/oswald -a-battle-martyr-11629728.html>.

21. Ibid.

22. Bede, Philip Hereford and Thomas Stapleton, *The Ecclesiastical History of the English People.* (London: Burns Oates & Washbourne, 1935).

23. Adams, Max, *The King in the North: The Life and Times of Oswald of Northumbria* (Head of Zeus, 2013).

24. "Oswald of Northumbria." *Wikipedia.* Wikimedia Foundation, 11 June 2014. Web. 07 Nov. 2014. <http:// en.wikipedia.org/wiki/Oswald_of_Northumbria>.

25. Rhodes, Bennie. *Christopher Columbus, Discoverer of America* (Milford, MI: Mott Media, 1976), 68.

26. "Columbus and His Creator." *Columbus and His Creator.* N.p., n.d. Web. 07 Nov. 2014. <http://www .icr.org/article/columbus-his-creator/>.

27. Federer, William J., *America's God and Country: Encyclopedia of Quotations* (Amerisearch, 2000), 113.

28. Irving, Washington, *The Life and Voyages of Christopher Columbus.* (Boston: Twayne, 1981).

29. "Medieval Sourcebook: Christopher Columbus: Extracts from Journal." *Internet History Sourcebooks Project.* N.p., n.d. Web. 05 Nov. 2014. <http://www .fordham.edu/halsall/source/columbus1.asp>.

30. Van Voorst, Robert, *Readings in Christianity* (Belmont, CA: Wadsworth/Thomson Learning, 2001), 175.

31. *Finding God, 19.*

32. Schmidt, Gary D., *William Bradford: Plymouth's Faithful Pilgrim* (Grand Rapids, MI: Wm. B. Eerdmans Publishing Co., 1999), 6.

33. *The Oregon Countryman*, Volume 4, Issues 2–3, October 1911, 36.

34. Carpenter, Edmund J. and Michael J. McHugh, ed., *Mayflower Pilgrims* (Christian Liberty Press, 2007), 74.

35. "Bay Psalm Book." *Wikipedia*. Wikimedia Foundation, 27 Oct. 2014. Web. 07 Nov. 2014. <http://en.wikipedia.org/wiki/Bay_Psalm_Book>.

36. Michael P. Clark, ed., *The Eliot Tracts: With Letters from John Eliot to Thomas Thorowgood and Richard Baxter* (Santa Barbara, CA: Praeger, 2003), 13.

37. Dyer, Edward O., *Gnadensee, the Lake of Grace; a Moravian Picture in a Connecticut Frame.* (Boston: Pilgrim, 1902), 19–20.

38. Ray, Edward C., "Thoughts for the Mid-week Hour of Prayer," *The New York Observer*, Volume 84: June 14, 1905, 7.

39. *The Eliot Tracts*, 122.

40. "John Eliot's Brief Narrative. 1909-14. American Historical Documents, 1000-1904. The Harvard Classics." *John Eliot's Brief Narrative. 1909-14. American Historical Documents, 1000-1904. The Harvard Classics.* N.p., n.d. Web. 07 Nov. 2014. <http://www.bartleby.com/43/12.html>.

41. "Susanna Wesley." *Wikipedia*. Wikimedia
    Foundation, 11 Feb. 2014. Web. 06 Nov. 2014. <http://
    en.wikipedia.org/wiki/Susanna_Wesley>.

42. Dengler, Sandy, *Susanna Wesley, Servant of God*
    (Chicago: Moody Publishers, 1987), 11.

43. "Susanna Wesley Thoughts on Raising Children."
    Prevailing Intercessory Prayer : Susanna Wesley. N.p.,
    n.d. Web. 06 Nov. 2014. <http://www.path2prayer.
    com/article/1042/revival-and-holy-spirit/books
    -sermons/new-resources/famous-christians-books
    -and-sermons/susanna-wesley-mother-of-methodism
    /susanna-wesley-child-raising-thoughts>.

44. Aitken, Jonathan, *John Newton: From Disgrace to
    Amazing Grace* (Wheaton, IL: Crossway, 2013).

45. "John Newton's Conversion." *John Newton's
    Conversion*. N.p., n.d. Web. 07 Nov. 2014. <http://
    grace-gospel.org/newton.htm>.

46. "Memoirs of John Newton." *Memoirs of John
    Newton*. N.p., n.d. Web. 07 Nov. 2014. <http://www
    .gracegems.org/Newton/Memoirs.htm>.

47. *Finding God*, 87.

48. Paull, Mrs. H.B., *Robert Raikes and His Scholars*,
    (Kessinger Publishing LLC), 15.

49. Gregory, Alfred, *Robert Raikes: Journalist and
    Philanthropist* (London: Hodder and Stoughton,
    1877), 50.

50. Ibid.

51. Paull, H. B., and C. Hewitt. *Robert Raikes and His
    Scholars. London: Sunday School Union, 1880,* 16.

52. Ibid.

53. "Robert Raikes." *Wikipedia*. Wikimedia Foundation, 11 June 2014. Web. 07 Nov. 2014. <http:// en.wikipedia.org/wiki/Robert_Raikes>.

54. Gregory, Alfred, *Robert Raikes: Journalist and Philanthropist. A History of the Origin of Sunday Schools.* (London: Hodder and Stoughton, 1877), 55.

55. "Robert Raikes and How We Got Sunday School." *Christianity.com*. N.p., n.d. Web. 13 Mar. 2015. <http://www.christianity.com/church/church -history/church-history-for-kids/robert-raikes-and-how -we-got-sunday-school-11635043.html>.

56. Ropes, Mary, "Mary Jones and Her Bible," *Sonlight Curriculum* (Littleston, CO: Sonlight, 2014), 11.

57. Ibid., 46.

58. Ibid., 57.

59. Ibid., 67.

60. "Mary Jones Took a Walk." *Christianity.com*. N.p., n.d. Web. 26 Jan. 2015. <http://www.christianity.com/ church/church-history/timeline/1701-1800/mary-jones -took-a-walk-11630335.html>.

61. "Mary Jones and Her Bible." *Wikipedia*. Wikimedia Foundation, n.d. Web. 27 Jan. 2015. <http:// en.wikipedia.org/wiki/Mary_Jones_and_her_Bible>.

62. "Sojourner Truth." *Wikipedia*. Wikimedia Foundation, 11 June 2014. Web. 07 Nov. 2014. <http:// en.wikipedia.org/wiki/Sojourner_Truth>.

63. Gilbert, Olive, *Sojourner Truth: Narrative of Sojourner Truth a Bondswoman of Olden Time* (Chicago: Johnson Publishing Company, 1970), 26.

64. Ibid., 27

65. Ibid., 44

66. Ibid., 45

67. Ibid., 47

68. Gilbert, Olive, and Sojourner Truth. *Narrative of Sojourner Truth.* (Mineola, NY: Dover Publications, 1997), 38.

69. "Isabella's Religious Experience." *The Narrative of Sojourner Truth, by Sojourner Truth; Page 6.* N.p., n.d. Web. 07 Nov. 2014. <http://www.page bypagebooks.com/Sojourner_Truth/The_Narrative _of_Sojourner_Truth/Isabellas_Religious_Experience _p6.html>.

70. "Catherine Booth | Christian History." *Catherine Booth | Christian History.* N.p., n.d. Web. 06 Nov. 2014. <http://www.christianitytoday.com/ch/ 131christians/activists/catherinebooth.html>.

71. Ibid.

72. Ibid.

73. Wiseman, Clarence D., *A Burning in My Bones: An Anecdotal Autobiography.* (Toronto: McGraw-Hill Ryerson, 1979), 130.

74. "Spartacus Educational." *Spartacus Educational.* N.p., n.d. Web. 27 Jan. 2015. <http://spartacus-educational. com>.

75. Ibid.

76. *Full Text of "The Life of Catherine Booth: The Mother of the Salvation Army"* N.p., n.d. Web. 06 Nov. 2014. <https://archive.org/stream/lifeofcatherineb01boot/ lifeofcatherineb01boot_djvu.txt>, 59.

77. Blaikie, William Garden, *The Personal Life of David Livingstone* (Ada, MI: Revell, 1880).

78. "David Livingstone." *Christian Biography Resources.* N.p., n.d. Web. 26 Jan. 2015. <http://wholesomewords .org/biography/biorplivingstone.html>.

79. "David Livingstone." *Wikipedia.* Wikimedia Foundation, 11 June 2014. Web. 07 Nov. 2014. <http:// en.wikipedia.org/wiki/David_Livingstone>.

80. Horne, C. Sylvester, *David Livingstone: Man of Prayer and Action* (Christian Liberty Press, 2007), xi.

81. "David Livingstone." *Wikipedia.*

82. Livingstone, David, *Missionary Travels and Researches in South Africa* (New York, 1858), 4–5.

83. *Finding God,* 119.

84. "Florence Nightingale, Nurse, Renewer of Society." *Florence Nightingale, Nurse, Renewer of Society.* N.p., n.d. Web. 07 Nov. 2014. <http://justus.anglican .org/resources/bio/158.html>.

85. Ibid.

86. Ibid.

87. "Florence Nightingale Pledge." *Florence Nightingale Pledge.* N.p., n.d. Web. 06 Nov. 2014. <http://nursing world.org/FunctionalMenuCategories/AboutANA/ WhereWeComeFrom/FlorenceNightingalePledge.aspx>.

88. "Florence Nightingale, Nurse, Renewer of Society."

89. "Florence Nightingale." *Wikipedia.* Wikimedia Foundation, 11 June 2014. Web. 06 Nov. 2014. <http:// en.wikipedia.org/wiki/Florence_Nightingale>.

90. "Answers to Prayer." *George Muller.* N.p., n.d. Web. 17 Mar. 2015. <http://www.wholesomewords.org/ biography/bmuller8.html>.

91. Steer, Roger, *George Muller: Delighted in God.* (Scotland, UK: Christian Focus Publications), 177.

92. Lawson, J. Gilchrist, *Deeper Experiences of Famous Christians*. (Anderson, IN: Warner Press, 1911).

93. "George Mueller, Orphanages Built by Prayer," *Chritianity.com*. N.p., n.d. Web 09 Mar. 2015. <http://www.christianity.com/church/church-history/church-history-for-kids/george-mueller-orphanages-built-by-prayer-11634869.html>.

94. "George Müller, Prayer Warrior, Founder of the Bristol Orphanage." *Path2Prayer.com*. N.p., n.d. Web 19 March 2015. <http://www.path2prayer.com/article/965/revival-and-holy-spirit/books-sermons/new-resources/famous-christians-books-and-sermons/george-mller-founder-of-bristol-orphanage>.

95. "George Müller." *Wikipedia*. Wikimedia Foundation, n.d. Web. 17 Mar. 2015. <http://en.wikipedia.org/wiki/George_M%C3%BCller>.

96. *George Muller: Delighted in God*, 177.

97. "Quotes." *Quotes*. N.p., n.d. Web. 17 Mar. 2015. <http://www.georgemuller.org/quotes.html>.

98. "George Müller « RE:quest." *REquest*. N.p., n.d. Web. 17 Mar. 2015. <http://request.org.uk/people-places/significant-people/2013/07/26/george-muller/>.

99. "GEORGE MULLER." *Lights 4 God*. N.p., 27 Sept. 2013. Web. 17 Mar. 2015. <https://lights4god.wordpress.com/2013/09/27/george-muller/>.

100. *Finding God*, 172.

101. "The Sunday News." *How Billy Sunday Was Saved*. N.p., n.d. Web. 07 Nov. 2014. <http://www.billysunday.org/cgi-bin/dada/mail.cgi?flavor=archive;list=BillySunday;id=20070729175839>.

102. "Billy Sunday." *Wikipedia.* Wikimedia Foundation, 24
     Jan. 2015. Web 28 Jan. 2015. <http://en.wikipedia.org/
     wiki/Billy_Sunday>.

103. *Finding God, 171.*

104. "Billy Sunday." *Billy Sunday.* N.p., n.d. Web. 14 Mar.
     2015. <http://www.u-s-history.com/pages/h3877.html>.

105. "Billy Sunday." *New World Encyclopedia.* N.p.,
     n.d. Web. 17 Mar. 2015. <http://www.newworld
     encyclopedia.org/entry/Billy_Sunday>.

106. Willmington, H. L., *Willmington's Guide to the Bible*
     (Carol Stream, IL: Tyndale House Publishers, 2011).
     Retrieved October 18, 2007.

107. All quotations this section—*The Washingtonian,*
     Volume 2, No. 6, Nov. 25, 1893.

108. Yancey, Philip, *A Skeptic's Guide to Faith.* (Grand
     Rapids, MI: Zondervan, 2009), 59.

109. "Amy Carmichael -The Weapon of Prayer «
     Prayercentral.net." *Prayercentralnet RSS.* N.p., n.d.
     Web. 07 Nov. 2014. <http://prayercentral.net/inspire
     -me/profiles-of-prayer/amy-carmichael-the-weapon
     -of-prayer/>. Story adapted from: "Things As They
     Are; Mission Work In Southern India" by Amy
     Carmichael.

110. "Amy Carmichael -The Weapon of Prayer"

111. "Amy Carmichael." *Wikipedia.* Wikimedia Foundation,
     11 June 2014. Web. 07 Nov. 2014. <http://en.wikipedia
     .org/wiki/Amy_Carmichael>.

112. Carmichael, Amy, *Candles in the Dark: Letters of
     Amy Carmichael.* (Fort Washington, PA: Christian
     Literature Crusade, 1982).

113. Ford, Charles O. "A Brief History of the Diocese of Michigan." *Historical Magazine of the Protestant Episcopal Church* 12.1 (1943), 18–30.

114. Sheets, Dutch. *Ultimate Guide to Prayer: Three Bestsellers in One Volume.* (Ada, MI: Bethany House, 2013), 362.

115. "Praying John Hyde." *The Christian Broadcasting Network.* N.p., n.d. Web. 27 Jan. 2015. <http://www.cbn.com/spirituallife/PrayerAndCounseling/Intercession/praying_john_hyde.aspx>.

116. "Profiles In Prayer: Praying John Hyde." *Praying John Hyde.* N.p., n.d. Web. 07 Nov. 2014. <http://www.cbn.com/spirituallife/PrayerAndCounseling/Intercession/praying_john_hyde.aspx?option=print>.

117. "Praying John Hyde," *The Christian Broadcasting Network.* N.p., n.d. Web. 17 Mar. 2015. <http://www.cbn.com/spirituallife/PrayerAndCounseling/Intercessionpraying_john_hyde.aspx>.

118. Brown, Pauline A., *Jars of Clay: Ordinary Christians on an Extraordinary Mission in Southern Pakistan.* (South Hadley, MA: Doorlight Publications, 2006), 227.

119. "Mother Teresa." *Wikipedia.* Wikimedia Foundation, 22 Jan. 2015 Web. 28 Jan. 2015. <http://en.wikipedia.org/Mother_Teresa>.

120. "Mother Teresa of Calcutta." *Mother Teresa.* N.p., n.d. Web. 05 Nov. 2014. <http://www.catholic.org/clife/teresa/>.

121. "Mother Teresa."

122. "Mother Teresa's Daily Prayer." *Mother Teresa's Daily Prayer.* N.p., n.d. Web. 07 Nov. 2014. <http://www.americancatholic.org/features/teresa/prayer.asp>.

123. Baldwin, David. *Royal Prayer a Surprising History.* (London: Continuum, 2009), 89.

124. Lukacs, John. *Five Days in London, May 1940.* New Haven: Yale UP, 1999.

125. "Top 10 Greatest Military Blunders of World War II," *Toptenz.net.* N.p., n.d. Web. 17 Mar. 2015. <http://www.toptenz.net/top-10-greatest-military-blunders-of-world-war-ii.php>.

126. "About Corrie Ten Boom." *Jerusalem PRAYER TEAM : About The Hiding Place.* The Corrie Ten Boom Fellowship, n.d. Web. 04 Nov. 2014. <http://jerusalemprayerteam.org/corrietenboom.asp>.

127. Ten Boom, Corrie, John L. Sherrill, and Elizabeth Sherrill, *The Hiding Place.* (Washington Depot, CT: Chosen, 1971), 201.

128. Ibid.

129. Kafer, Donna, *Women of Courage.* (Orlando, FL: Bridge-Logos, 2007), 10.

130. Ten Boom, Corrie and Jamie Buckingham, *Tramp for the Lord.* (Fort Washington, PA: Christian Literature Crusade, 1974), 54.

131. Guideposts. "The Question of God: Corrie Ten Boom." *PBS.* PBS, n.d. Web. 04 Nov. 2014. <http://www.pbs.org/wgbh/questionofgod/voices/boom.html>.

132. Ten Boom, Corrie, *Clippings from My Notebook: Writings and Sayings Collected.* (Nashville: Thomas Nelson, 1982), 19.

133. *"Corrie Ten Boom: A Legacy of Courage,"* *Charisma Magazine.* N.p., n.d. Web. 17 Mar. 2015. <http://www.charismamag.com/spirit/devotionals/ by-love-transformed?view=article&id=9933%3Acor rie-ten-boom-a-legacy-of-courage&catid=24>.

134. Bethge, Eberhard, *Dietrich Bonhoeffer: A Biography* (Minneapolis: Fortress Press, 2000), 927.

135. Bonhoeffer, Dietrich, *Life Together: The Classic Exploration of Christian Community.* (New York: HarperOne, 2009), 17

136. Fedele, Gene, *Heroes of Faith* (Alachua, FL: Bridge Logos Publishing, 2003), 240.

137. Ibid.

138. Dietrich Bonhoeffer, *Life Together* (San Francisco: HarperSanFrancisco, 1954), 21.

139. "Dietrich Bonhoeffer." *Wikipedia.* Wikimedia Foundation, n.d. Web. 17 Mar. 2015. <http:// en.wikipedia.org/wiki/Dietrich_Bonhoeffer>.